SOLUTION FOCUSED GROUP THERAPY

IDEAS FOR GROUPS IN PRIVATE
PRACTICE, SCHOOLS, AGENCIES,
AND TREATMENT PROGRAMS

LINDA METCALF, Ph.D.

THE FREE PRESS

New York

THE FREE PRESS
A Division of Simon & Schuster Inc.
1230 Avenue of the Americas
New York, NY 10020

The FREE PRESS and colophon are trademarks
of Simon & Schuster Inc.

Designed by Michael Mendelsohn of MM Design 2000, Inc.

Manufactured in the United States of America

10   9   8   7   6   5   4   3   2   1

Library of Congress Cataloging-in-Publication Data

Metcalf, Linda.
    Solution focused group therapy: ideas for groups in private
practice, schools, agencies, and treatment programs/Linda Metcalf.
        p.   cm.
    Includes bibliographical references and index.
    1. Group psychotherapy. 2. Solution-focused therapy. 3. Brief
psychotherapy.   I. Title.
RC488.M48   1998
616.89'152—dc21   98–26800
                                                      CIP

ISBN 0-684-84744-2

This book is dedicated to my family,
Roger Jr., Kelli, Ryan, and Roger Sr.,
my personal support group.

CONTENTS

FOREWORD

Throughout the years, group therapy has experienced an on and off recognition by psychotherapists. Despite these surges in popularity, group therapy has remained a method chosen by the few, not the many.

Today, economic conditions, and a new emphasis on strengths and resiliency in psychotherapy, are creating a very strong climate for group work. The economic climate for therapists has become so tight that they have had to explore new methods to make each hour more profitable. Since third-party payers are encouraging group therapy, and more money can be made per hour, it is natural for clinicians to engage in group therapy.

Therapists who use a solution focused therapy approach clearly understand how a group can almost exponentially increase potential solutions to presented problems. In addition, a group that focuses on strengths and resources simply feels better to both a clinician and client. Similar to watching a child make a playful and exciting discovery, solution focused group therapy creates an environment where clients become excited about discovering hidden strengths and unrecognized internal solutions.

This increased utilization of the group therapy format is also creating some exciting changes regarding how group therapy is delivered. This book is an excellent example of some of those changes. While solution focused therapy has gained recognition for its work with individuals, little attention has been given to its use in group therapy formats.

Originally, solution focused therapy was met with a great deal of resistance due to the assumptions, concepts, and methods that challenged traditional psychotherapy values. While I hope such resistance does not meet solution focused group therapy, it is quite likely that a similar dynamic will occur for those who begin to learn and apply these principles to more traditional therapy group populations. Linda Metcalf does an exceptional job of explaining how to create, or transition, to a solution focused group therapy format. However, some ideas will clearly challenge a more traditional position. I encourage you to read through these areas and approach this information with an open mind.

From beginning to end, Linda does a nice job of demonstrating the differences between a solution focused group and a nonsolution focused group. Through clinical examples, case studies, and transcriptions, Linda thoroughly explains the necessary shifts needed to create a solution focused atmosphere. Particularly useful are the worksheets she offers to assist the client and clinician struggling to make such transitions.

Some clinicians will struggle with the change of emphasis to abilities, exceptions, and strengths from the deficit- and pathology-based models. Chapter 3, "Disease Versus Habit," is an excellent education on this shift, highlighting practical methods to change the tone of the sessions and move toward a solution focused approach to group therapy.

The range of clinical populations covered in this book demonstrates the utility of solution focused therapy. Too often, therapists attempt to negate a new style of therapy because they feel the population they treat is "different," explaining that the particular therapy just cannot be done with "these clients." Linda clearly demonstrates that clinicians, when they understand the principles of solution focused therapy, can apply them to any group format. I found Chapter 8, "Solution Focused Groups Unlimited," to be very poignant. This chapter emphatically demonstrates that solution focused therapy is much more than a set of techniques or gimmicks—it is a therapist's way of thinking about problems and clients. While techniques can be superficial and trite, the true value of solution focused therapy is in the epistemology by which a therapist approaches therapy. Once this shift is made, solution focused therapy can occur with any clinical population.

The clear "how-to" strategies are a major strength of this book. While these strategies appear relatively easy, Linda also explains how difficult it can be to implement the ideas and techniques. She offers strategies to some common roadblocks when implementing solution focused techniques. Another invigorating area pertained to the ideas and strategies offered by leaders in the field using solution focused group principles outside the therapy room (Chapter 9). This creativity refreshingly demonstrates that therapists can blend their personal style and interests with solution focused concepts.

Conceptually, clinicians will say, "This makes sense." Pragmatically, there will be moments when clinicians will feel, "This group can't do solution focused therapy." These are the moments in which therapists need to stay focused and place their trust in the model. The group will hold a vast amount of resources and natural solutions; however, clinicians need to learn that the group members hold the answers to one another's problems, not always the therapist.

I encourage you to kick back and take in the wonderful ideas presented by Linda. Most importantly, please consider how you can get out of the way of your clients' becoming experts in identifying their strengths. Allow them to utilize the surplus of ideas presented in a solution focused group therapy session to develop their own solutions.

—Tracy Todd, Ph.D.
President
Brief Therapy Institute
of Denver

ACKNOWLEDGMENTS

Over the past four years I have been blessed with editors who have listened to my ideas and have given me opportunities to share them with you. The first two books were challenging and exciting to write, and my purpose in writing them was to offer new ideas for parents and educators so that children could experience a better way to live and to learn. This book was more difficult to write. Facilitating therapy in groups of people instead of individuals has been fun to do but difficult to describe. In preparing this manuscript I found myself at first burdened by the need to follow the theories surrounding solution focused brief therapy and inhibited by my attempts to sound politically correct. It was hard to be creative when the theory monopolized the tone.

When my editor, Philip Rappaport, commented on how this manuscript differed in tone from the first two books, I realized that I had strayed from what I adore about solution focused brief therapy—the spontaneous discovery of solutions that can never be produced by specific techniques or questions. I remembered Bill O'Hanlon's wise comment that therapy needs to be light because life itself is too drudging and my friend Brian Cade's belief that we as therapists influence our clients not only in what we do and say but in what we think. Then the book came together. These recollections helped me to reexperience the initial excitement I felt for solution focused brief therapy and to focus on what it is in group conversations that creates spontaneous solutions. Wisdom is always hidden within the individuals in each group, and the group therapy interactions are what help to bring it to life. This is what makes the groups work, not the model. Thank you, Philip, for recognizing what worked for me before!

I also appreciate having had the opportunity to work with so many group members who have proven to me over and over that introducing a new focus to a group can assist its members in discovering something new to focus on in their lives. They have taught me that the potential for self-discovery that lies within each of us is there for the taking. A special thanks to my colleagues Karen Rayter, Michael Bishop, Ben Furman, Brian Cade, Stephen Chilton, Ruth Readyhough, Scot Cooper, Janet Roth, Christina Hayes, and Blaine Powel for their ideas and enthusiasm. Their contributions show how solution focused brief therapy can be applied in creative ways when therapists look across the therapy room for something besides problems and do something new to discover their clients' strengths. And finally, with much sincerity and appreciation, I acknowledge the efforts of my husband, Roger, whose confidence in what I do encourages me daily. His efforts in helping to copyedit this book have made it more reader friendly.

If you are a new therapist or someone new to solution focused brief therapy, I thank you for giving me an opportunity to free your mind of theoretical jargon for a few hundred pages and to show you what *can* happen when a group of people get together with a therapist who has a new orientation. Sit back and read about the experiences of people who came together to converse about their problems and found a better way to solve them by looking at times in their lives when their problems were less severe. Read on about how they discovered through their own and through others' observations that things *had* progressed and that they had simply been off track temporarily. Allow their discoveries to take you to a place where therapy knows no limits or rules and where the solution to each individual's problem is always unique.

—Linda Metcalf

1 Changing Directions in Group Therapy

Even if you're on the right track,
you'll get run over if you just sit there.

—Will Rogers

The adolescents in the early morning process group stumbled into the group therapy room. Some of the kids dove toward the large pillows on the floor; the rest reluctantly approached and flopped onto the couches. The tech (mental health technician or MHT) followed them in, flipped through his roll sheets, found their names, and attempted to gain their attention by threatening them. Those who listened were acknowledged, and those who did not listen were asked to move closer to the tech. For the most part, the teens stared at me, wondering what they would be expected to do that day. I looked at them and noticed their reluctance to be there.

It was a typical Monday morning in 1990 at a local psychiatric facility in Texas. Here I facilitated group treatment for various mental health problems, such as chemical dependency, anger, dysfunctional family dynamics, sexual abuse, and depression. I had used such theoretical models as strategic therapy, structural therapy, and family-of-origin therapy in running the groups, orienting each group session around what the treatment team deemed helpful to the patients. On that Monday morning I decided to try something new. I wanted to begin integrating into the context of the adolescent group some of the solution focused brief therapy ideas I was currently using in individual therapy sessions. I had set up a video camera in the corner of the room beforehand so that I could view the entire process later. Some of the teens seemed to be surprised and caught off guard when I began the group with a different type of question than what they were used to. "Look

1

back over the weekend and tell me what seemed to go slightly better for each of you," I said.

Silence. It was the kind of silence where you wonder if you're speaking some alien language. I was thankful when, after a few minutes and a repetition of the question, Dylan spoke:

> Well, I visited my family on Sunday, and we did not fight. That's good for them but bad for me. When I got back here last night, one of the techs asked how things went, and when I told him, he said I stuffed my feelings and that if I kept it up, eventually I would probably explode again. That's how it always is. I go along and do okay until my old man does something stupid, and then I blow up. That's how I got sent here.

LM: So, Dylan, was this the first time you were able to not fight?

DYLAN: Since I've been in here it is.

LM: You know, you said someone called it stuffing your feelings. I think it sounds as if you just self-disciplined yourself.

DYLAN: [Stares, without commenting]

LM: In fact, I'm quite impressed with you. I wonder what your parents would say they noticed about you while you were self-disciplining yourself this weekend.

DYLAN: Everybody seemed to have a pretty good time. It was quiet. We actually talked without anybody getting too mad. It was pretty different.

LM: Did anyone in the group happen to see Dylan when he came back last night from his visit?

SUSIE: I did. He seemed cool. His parents didn't look mad like they usually do.

TOM: Yeah, I'm his roommate. He seemed okay. Usually he comes back upset, but last night he was better.

DYLAN: But isn't it bad if I keep on stuffing these feelings and don't say what I need to tell my parents when they make me mad?

LM: I don't know. What usually works best for you, telling them how you feel and getting mad or self-disciplining yourself like you did last weekend and somehow talking to them calmly?

DYLAN: Self-disciplining myself.

The adolescent process group was part of an inpatient treatment program, and the clients were assigned to the group by a treatment team consisting of a psychiatrist, a case manager, a nurse, and a psychologist. The patients also received individual therapy so that they could have personal time to discuss intimate issues. The group therapy component was added so that patients could learn how similar issues had affected others and how they were solving them. For the most part, the group sessions focused on confronting substance abusers and talking about recovery, describing sexual abuse experiences, toning down angry outbursts, discussing the effects of depression, or learning about unhealthy relationships. These sessions were a continuation of individual therapy, but in group therapy a problem focus was used as a theoretical basis.

I continued to facilitate the adolescent group process with a solution focused approach for the next few weeks, always beginning the group with the same type of question and *always* looking for what was going better in the group members' lives. Dylan became one of my more outspoken group members, often interrupting other members to remind them to self-discipline themselves. The tech began to remark how this morning process group was easier to manage than the other groups and how the kids talked about how much they liked it because I seemed to like them. I noticed that several of the kids in the group who were previously referred to as "sleepers" had begun to talk more and to sit on chairs rather than on pillows. Some teens even moved to sit closer to me. Most seemed better able to recall issues they were working on each week, and the war stories decreased drastically. I was sold.

THE SOLUTION FOCUSED VERSUS THE PROBLEM-FOCUSED GROUP

The wise don't expect to find life worth living; they make it that way.

—Anonymous

In psychodynamic group therapy, members reveal their issues, express their unhappiness or distraught feelings, relate to and confront others who feel as despondent as they do, and search for insight that might lead to new behaviors and actions. Over the years, I have learned from many clients that while these groups are supportive, they are also unproductive, continuing for months and sometimes years on end and focusing just on what went wrong in the past. Clients emerge from those groups with insight yet wearing their hearts on their sleeves and ready to rationalize and defend why they had their particular disorders or complaints. There seemed to be few actual strategies that developed within those groups; instead, psychodynamic therapists offered so-called proven strategies that were described as "the way to recovery." When clients returned to a group session without having tried such strategies, they were considered "not ready to change" or "resistant." (Some clients have told me that they often left such groups feeling worse than when they began attending them.)

When changing the direction of group therapy by integrating a solution focused approach, it is important for the therapist to give group members new ideas with which to construct new stories and to discourage them from adding to the pathological dialogue. For example, the change of atmosphere in the aforementioned adolescent group seemed to guide group members into more productive conversations, with more solution-friendly attitudes. However, the change took time and constant coaching and redirecting on my part to keep group members on a solution track instead of a problem track. Normally, the teens were told what they needed to do by the technicians and therapists. Dylan, for example, was told not to "stuff" his feelings. He previously lacked the confidence and self-awareness to understand his own competency, making him dependent on staff to solve his problems. Treatment was typically prolonged, since clients were not discharged until they performed the behaviors the treatment team decided they *should* perform. I offered Dylan an opportunity to become the sole expert on his life. This was a new process that sparked his curiosity and interest and pushed his participation to the next level. He began to respect himself in an environment that promoted such respect. When the group took a new direction, Dylan's apparent change of attitude, his new self-respect and positive beliefs about himself, became contagious.

I believe that people enjoy being part of a solution focused process group primarily because it helps them find a comfortable place in the world, one in which their problems do not seem to take over. Such a safe experience offers an oasis to even the most despondent client. Despondent clients are more likely to give up their pathological descriptions when they discover that such descriptions are not going to be discussed. Instead, clients are invited to revisit the past and reminisce about the times when life was better. This experience often has the same uplifting effect as looking at old photographs of loved ones. As clients recall more pleasant times, they realize that life was not always so difficult; as each member hears others make this discovery, a kinship develops within the group, creating an atmosphere of hope. As clients realize that they have had successes in life, whether in the past or in dealing with a current situation, they seem to enjoy the idea that others, namely, fellow group members, have noticed such success. In solution focused group therapy sessions, the group helps to define the direction for its members to follow, validating and giving permission to each member to try new strategies.

A BRIEF HISTORY OF SOLUTION FOCUSED BRIEF THERAPY

If you are not part of the solution, you are part of the problem.
—Eldridge Cleaver

Traditionally, when clients came to therapy, they did so with a desire to understand how their lives went wrong. They looked to therapists to give them explanations in the hope that understanding the root of the problem would tell them what to do differently in order to correct the problem. Thus, therapists oriented themselves in the past instead of the present and searched for why problems occurred, that is, for information they could give their clients. For some action-oriented clients, such explanations motivated them enough to try the strategies handed down to them by their therapists. For other clients, such explanations gave them more reasons to feel and act incompetent. When Milton Erickson began working with clients in the mid 1950's, he took a new approach to therapy, one that offered new ideas for therapists to consider. "He addressed himself consistently to the fact that individuals have a reservoir of wisdom learned and forgotten but still available. He suggested that his patients explore alternative ways of organizing their experience without exploring the etiology or dynamics or the dysfunction" (Minuchin & Fishman, 1981, pp. 268–269).

With this new approach emerged a new sort of client: one who could leave therapy with identified tools to solve future problems independently. The therapist became someone who helped the client access these resources and put them into use. This respectful stance became one of the basic constructs of solution focused brief therapy. However, the solution focused approach was still years away, even though a brief therapy was emerging on the West Coast.

At the Mental Research Institute, John Weakland, Richard Fisch, Paul Watzlawick, and others worked with clients within a time limit of ten sessions. Their purpose was to reorganize the thinking of clients instead of trying to promote insight. In the view of the therapists at MRI, problems occur when the actions in life are mishandled. The greater the effort a person makes to try to solve the problem through inappropriate actions, the more entrenched the problem becomes and the less responsibility the person takes to solve it. The problem-focused approach involves thinking that problems are interactional and can best be solved when clients do something different around the problem.

In the 1980s, solution focused brief therapy took a different turn in reference to how problems are viewed. Steve de Shazer and his team at the Brief Family Therapy Center in Milwaukee began looking at "what has been working in order to identify and amplify these solution sequences" (de Shazer, 1982, 1985). In this approach, the recognition that a client's problems do not *constantly* occur encouraged therapists to focus on those problem-absent times as *exceptions* and to investigate which features of those times could be used in constructing a solution to the presenting problem. By identifying the specific interactions, behaviors, and thinking that helped them in past situations, clients were more apt to regard themselves as competent and to realize that they could solve their own problems with minimal assistance. Therapeutic tasks began to develop from these exceptions that clients presented to their therapist. The therapist's task became one of creating opportunities for clients to see themselves as competent and resourceful. Sometimes that meant asking a client to observe for a few days the times when the problem occurred less often; other times the client was to carry out small, specific tasks that he identified as helpful in dissolving the problem. With these new, less intrusive actions, the therapist assumed a less directive role. In believing that clients are the expert on their own life, the solution focused therapist became a sort of facilitator, guide, or assistant to the client; the purpose of such a therapist was to create opportunities for clients to see themselves as the expert on their own life.

ASSUMPTIONS FOR FACILITATING SOLUTION FOCUSED GROUP THERAPY

People gather into groups to discuss their situations and to learn from each other new perceptions and ways of thinking that may influence their solutions for living. In solution focused groups, the focus of the conversation is on those times when a group member's problem is *not* a problem. The beauty of such groups emerges when members observe how others are able to discover such problem-free times, motivating them to try and find such discoveries within themselves. When group members participate in this collaborative process, the strategies grow geometrically. The result? Group conversations become even more efficient in promoting discussion of problem-free times and clients become more action oriented.

To explore the differences between problem-focused and solution focused group therapy, I will discuss several basic ideas adapted from the solution focused assumptions offered by O'Hanlon and Weiner-Davis in their book *In Search of Solutions* (1989, pp. 34–50). These numbered points are guidelines for the solution focused therapist to use during group therapy.

1. *Keep the group nonpathological, redescribing problems to open up possibilities.*

When group members describe themselves and their lives with a problem focus or a diagnosis, these descriptions continue to reinforce their beliefs about themselves, keeping them stuck in old actions. I have observed this situation particularly in groups for persons who were abused sexually. Group members may complain and express frustration over either their inability to be intimate sexually or emotionally because of the trauma or their inability to stop their promiscuous actions. These feelings are well founded and should command a therapist's respect. However, a therapist who validates these feelings may provide such group members with an explanation that will serve only to reinforce their destructive actions. The negative behaviors that trouble such clients may then become part of their personal belief system about themselves, thus discouraging any chance for escaping from the trauma and moving toward intimacy.

When group members label themselves in such a problem-focused or pathological manner, I have found it helpful to offer a new description that invites them to think about the exceptions. Many people enter group therapy because it was mandated by a court or because it was suggested by their individual therapist or physician. Every client's diagnosis is important and should be respected for its purpose in defining the underlying fact that something has gone astray. However, according to Michael White (1990), "Since the stories that persons have about their lives determine both the ascription of meaning to experience and the selection of those aspects of experience that are to be given expression, these stories are constitutive of shaping the persons' lives. The lives and relationships of persons evolve as they live through or perform these stories" (p. 40).

As members each describe the situation that brings them to the group, the solution focused group leader will kindly and respectfully suggest to each member a new description that employs hope. This is more easily understood after clients have had a chance to describe what they think the group needs to know about them. White refers to a need for redescription of disorders or complaints. Below are examples of how problems can be redescribed to create new perceptions:

Problem Description	New Solution Perception
Eating disorder	A *habit* of eating/not eating certain foods that influences your health in a negative manner
Major depression	A feeling of *sadness* that evolves from a sad turn of events
Hyperactivity	*Energy* that interferes with calmness, rest, or relationships
Anger disorder	A feeling of being angry that is at times *justified* but that you forget to control in a way that is acceptable to others
Bipolar disorder	*Mood swings* that tend to keep you from being calm, organized, and collected
Anxiety attacks	A tendency to *act out your fears* in a physical way that interferes with the activities you want to try/do

Suggesting a new perception does not change the diagnosis or minimize the problem. The new perception simply *normalizes* and *redefines* the presenting problem so that the group member begins to perceive solutions to it. O'Hanlon and Weiner-Davis (1989) describe the positive effects of normalizing as follows: "If pressed to speculate about the cause of many difficulties that motivate people to seek therapy, we would say that these difficulties have come about from some random events that just stuck around long enough to become viewed as a problem. We tend to view these things not as pathological manifestations, but as ordinary difficulties of life" (p. 93).

2. Focus on exceptions to the problems discussed in group interactions.

Exceptions are real events that occur outside of the problem context. In solution focused individual therapy the only observers of competency are the therapist and client. In group therapy the audience widens and more input is available. The following are examples of questions the therapist can ask in an effort to identify when problems do *not* occur and what group members do to accomplish these nonproblem times:

Can you recall ways that you have handled disagreements more constructively?

What is different about the times when you do not feel quite as depressed?

Can you share with the group what you did when you successfully resisted the urge to drink?

Changing the direction in therapy from problem focus to solution focus can dramatically change the beliefs of clients and motivate them in even the most dire of circumstances. The following case study is an example of what can happen in a person's life when a new description of a problem is offered (this client began in individual therapy and then continued the treatment process later in group therapy):

Annette was grief stricken from a failed marriage, overwhelmed by the responsibility of having full custody of a rambunctious four-year-old, and worried about her twenty-year-old son, who had been arrested for using and selling drugs, and her twenty-four-year-old daughter, whose marriage had also failed. Annette had attempted suicide three times within the year by overdosing with prescribed medications. Her first attempt occurred shortly after her son left his second treatment center and her daughter filed for divorce and moved back home. Over a period of several months, Annette attended inpatient and then outpatient therapy, but she continued in her hopeless view of life. She made a second suicide attempt, believing that even her four-year-old son would be "better off." She had learned in her inpatient therapy that she was the daughter her mother never loved and the problem coworker who was a "pain in the neck." More pathologizing led to more self-pity, and Annette attempted to take her life for the third time.

A coworker of hers made Annette's first appointment at my office after the third suicide attempt and accompanied her to the first session. By the time I met Annette, she had been in and out of a psychiatric facility for several months. (She was discharged each time with more medication for her depression, plus sleeping medication as well!) It truly seemed that Annette had the weight of the world on her shoulders. As I began to work with her, she would often remind me that no matter what happened next, she wouldn't be surprised; she had lived through practically everything. I agreed with her that it seemed that way. I was also interested in what her other therapists had done that was helpful. She replied, "They just listened for the most part. Their suggestions never really made sense to me because they had no idea where I was in my mind."

Before I invited Annette into group therapy, we spent several sessions in individual therapy exploring the days and times when she did not overdose. This was a different experience for Annette. She had received assertiveness and coping training in her inpatient treatment, but these approaches apparently did not fit with her personality; thus, she never used the techniques offered in the training sessions. When she failed at carrying out the tasks assigned to her, she felt hopeless and again began having suicidal thoughts.

I realized that I needed to step aside and not lead Annette. She had been led before and had rejected the direction. Instead, I encouraged her to focus on those times when she did not rely on medication to relieve her emotional pain. This took time and required many compliments from me on her ability to cope even slightly under these most stressful situations, situations she did not quite understand. Eventually, in individual therapy, we found that she felt less hopeless when she had social plans, such as a night out with girlfriends, a few hours of shopping, a brief trip, or lunch at her parents' house. I began to recognize at this point that the social setting of a therapy group might be helpful to her. Annette began to learn that her mother's and sister's influence on her lessened when she was assertive with them in a kind manner more fitting to her personality. Her new confidence eventually was recognized by her ex-husband, who began paying child support on a more regular basis when Annette learned to insist on a deadline.

    3. When you notice a group member's competency in the group process, comment on it intermittently and gather other group members' thoughts on your discovery.

    A year after her first suicide attempt, Annette was finally no longer giving in to the destructive thoughts that had overwhelmed her on so many occasions. Now, with less medication in her medicine cabinet, she took walks when she felt stressed, instead of attempting to take her life. I asked Annette to become a part of a newly formed women's group. In her first group session she made few comments, except for telling her story briefly. Before the meeting ended, I said to the group, "I have a favor to ask. I would like you each to think about the stories you have heard tonight and share an idea or two with each other regarding some strengths you might have noticed in each other."

    After a few moments, several of the group members gave each other compliments. Annette sat quietly. Finally, a group member addressed Annette's bravery in withstanding an ordeal she had had with her older son; she remembered how difficult it had been for her to watch her own daughter follow the path of alcoholism. She told Annette that no matter what anyone would ever say about her, she was a truly loving parent who never gave up on her son. She said that as Annette talked about her son, she could see that she was concerned about him and yet able to set boundaries with him.

The next group began with my usual question: "What went slightly better last week?" When solution focused groups meet for the first few times, members often have difficulty with this question, because it directs them toward solution talk when their assumption is that group therapy means coming to admit their faults and limitations. Instead of encouraging members to commiserate with each other, this question stretches their awareness of themselves and encourages them to notice the good days. Therapists may at first find themselves often redirecting the conversation toward solution perceptions; however, after the first two or three meetings, the atmosphere becomes more natural and group clients begin to partake in solution talk more readily.

Annette had come in telling jokes during this second meeting, thus gaining the confidence of the group and helping to lighten the tone of the meeting. Now she responded to my question:

"I've had one of the worst weeks ever. My boss thought I was resigning from my job when I gave him a letter of concern about my job description, and for about three days I had no job! Then I got rehired in another department. I think my son is doing something crazy again, but I didn't do any funny stuff this time. Instead, we just got down and talked. He's still at home, my daughter's left her husband again and come home again, and I still think I will never be alone. So I'm going out on Friday night this weekend, and if any of you want to go with me, hey, I'm ready."

What occurred to change Annette's belief in herself? I'm not sure that it matters! For the next several weeks, she came to group meetings and shared her insights about the others' abilities. On several occasions she said to a group member, "Look at me. If I can do this, anyone can do this."

The power of noticing a person's ability *on the spot* keeps the compliments real. Otherwise, the feedback can seem fake and contrived, and group clients may have trouble switching personal definitions of themselves. For example, Judy, an adolescent girl who viewed herself as ugly, nonsocial, and strange, once spoke up in a girls' group about being and feeling so "different." After Judy shared how odd she often felt when talking to others, I asked the group to describe to her how she seemed to come across when she talked to them. As each group member conveyed approval of her conversational abilities, Judy sat back, aghast. She then said that her mother often reprimanded her for appearing strange and that she had come to believe that her mother was correct. I then suggested to the group that perhaps they could help her show her mother the seemingly normal personality we were noticing. Judy was pleased and accepted these ideas readily.

> 4. *Avoid any tendency to promote insight and instead focus on the client's ability to survive the problem situation.*

Neff Blackmon, Ph.D., a marriage and family therapist who facilitates inpatient chemical dependency recovery groups, started using a solution focused approach in his private practice with groups of women who had survived sexual abuse. Although many of his clients had attended sexual abuse therapy groups for years, within a few weeks the women were dropping out of group therapy because they felt so much better. Instead of having them talk about the sad, unfortunate details of the abuse, Blackmon had encouraged them to focus on survivorship. While some group members needed what he referred to as a "running start" (i.e., the opportunity to talk briefly about the incidents that had happened to them), most of his clients found his approach refreshing, and some said they felt less violated by not having to recall the details of past events.

His new focus also seemed to help group members watch for the successes (no matter how small) in their lives. He promoted this by asking questions such as the following:

> If you no longer had to come here or couldn't come here to therapy anymore, how would I know things were better by what you did versus what you said?

If you were doing the right things for yourself during the next week and I pretended to be Martin Scorsese, filming you when you did those things, what would you point out to me to film?

Another strategy that Blackmon used to help group members see themselves differently was to take them on field trips to baseball batting cages. His suspicions were that many group members needed a chance to have a physical outlet for expressing their feelings in healthy, strenuous, and "appropriately violent" ways. Once group members began to enjoy these activities, they began doing other activities together outside of group time. In Blackmon's words, "they learned to have fun instead of just being miserable." Encouraging new behaviors by providing group members with a dramatically different type of experience is a novel way of assisting them in discovering alternative ways of living and coping.

Blackmon tells the story of one group member, Jody, the wife of a pilot, who cleaned up her garage and bought a cheap set of dishes at a discount store. She and a friend then went into the garage and threw the dishes, breaking them into pieces. "I was never allowed to be angry about the stuff that happened to me," she said. Blackmon was so impressed by her determination to live her life differently that he asked her these questions: "What other signs would there be for the wife of a captain of an airline that would say that she had it together?" "If I didn't see you again for a year and I ran into you somewhere after that year, how would I know you were better?"

The woman began flying to Paris at least once a month to have fun and enjoy herself. What made a difference for her in the group setting? Blackmon momentarily stepped into her world and stimulated her to think of new ideas that were readily available to her. The strategy Blackmon used was important, since it did not force or require his clients to do things that were too out of the ordinary for them. I strongly caution therapists to refrain from urging their clients to engage in totally unfamiliar activities. Clients seem to be more likely to take on activities that are comfortable for them and in which they have some expertise. For Jody, flying was available and something she had done before; the experience seemed to provide her with an avenue of escape from the past.

> 5. *Attempt to see group members as people who have com-
> plaints about their lives, not as persons with symptoms.*

The beliefs we carry around about people enter the therapy room with us. The therapist's empathy, compassion, and concern for others is important, but in solution focused group therapy what is especially important is the ability to make clients understand that they have strengths and coping mechanisms and have had past success in troublesome situations. Such a message provides clients with a feeling of relief, a feeling that can evolve into positive attitudes which then can result in productive actions. For example:

- When Blackmon took his group to the batting cages, the message became "You can do this; you can have fun even though this trauma occurred in your life."
- When Dylan thought of himself as self-disciplined, the message was "I've been successful but I didn't realize it before; I can stay calm with my dad."
- Because she heard a message of "You're okay" from group members, Judy felt normal in the eyes of her peers and was more likely to try normal behaviors at home.
- When Annette was described as having incredible coping abilities, she received a message that she could do something more constructive than rely on medication to solve her problem.

These discoveries were made by the clients themselves, but it was their group who gathered together and set the stage for the discoveries that changed their beliefs. When we therapists think of ourselves as stage directors helping actors stand in places on a stage where their talents are best noticed and utilized, we see how powerful the competency-based statements are that we use to coax our reluctant actors into new roles. The trick lies, therefore, in our own methods of discovering our clients' abilities.

The following exercise can help you identify how you think about clients. It can orient you toward looking only for strengths in a client who is in a chaotic situation and can be used as a beginning exercise with a new group. It was developed and presented by Tracy Todd, Ph.D., in his manual *Brief Therapy Workbook of Exercises and Role Plays* (1996, p. 13). I have changed the format slightly for the group setting.

EXERCISE

Divide the therapy group into two groups. Tell both groups that you will all be watching the first ten minutes of the movie *Home Alone*. Ask one group to watch for all of the problems in the family, and ask the other group to watch for the family strengths. After viewing the movie, draw a line down the center of a chalkboard and label one side *strengths* and the other side *weaknesses*. Notice which side has the most descriptions. Discuss how easy it is to label problems and how difficult it can be to identify strengths during chaotic times. Then ask these questions:

> If we brought this family in for consultation with us, which descriptions would give them direction? Why?

> Can those of you who manage to see strengths amidst the chaos give us an idea as to how you did this?

> If just for a week you all used what we've talked about to see strengths in your own family, what would you suggest that you could think about when times at home become chaotic?

This exercise tends to shed light on the power of focusing on something new and different and on the actions that emerge when we do so. It is a positive way to show the impact of talking to someone about their abilities and not their deficits. An additional exercise for therapists to use after this activity has been performed is described below:

Ask group members to form partners by facing the person next to them. Ask the partners to choose between themselves one partner who will pretend to be very troubled by something that is occurring in the relationship. The other partner will pretend to be content with the relationship.

PART ONE: COMPLAINING

Begin the exercise by asking the troubled partner to complain in detail for the next five minutes to the other partner everything that is wrong between them. After the process has taken place, ask each of the partners who received the complaining to describe the emotions that they felt during the process and what resolutions were made.

PART TWO: REMINISCING

Ask the partners to keep the same roles. Instruct the troubled partners to turn to the other partner and describe in detail how troubled they are and then to share for five minutes with their partners the more successful times in the relationship. Encourage the troubled partners to go into specific details of what has worked before in the relationship.

Watch the atmosphere and the noise level change between the first and second exercise. After allowing time for the partners to converse, ask the group members who pretended to be the troubled partners to describe which scenario was more satisfying. Ask the other partners to describe their experiences of being complained to and then shared with.

6. *Remember that complex problems do not necessarily require complex solutions. This is the time to assist your group therapy clients to think in simpler ways.*

In *The Seven Habits of Highly Effective People* (1989), Stephen Covey quotes Erich Fromm as an astute observer of the roots and fruits of the Personality Ethic:

Today we come across an individual who behaves like an automaton, who does not know or understand himself, and the only person that he knows is the person that he is supposed to be, whose meaningless chatter has replaced communicative speech, whose synthetic smile has replaced genuine laughter, and whose sense of dull despair has taken the place of genuine pain. Two statements may be said concerning this individual. One is that he suffers from defects of spontaneity and individuality that may seem to be incurable. At the same time it may be said for him he does not differ essentially from the millions of the rest of us who walk upon the earth. (Fromm, as quoted by Covey, p. 36)

I like this passage for two reasons. The first is that it normalizes group members who have difficulty in focusing on what is working in their lives and helps them feel a sort of membership with others who simply have a difficult time seeing their personal strengths. It is difficult to go through a tough day and at the end of it just focus on those actions that *did* work. The solution focused group therapist must consider how difficult this recognition can be and remain patient with group members who continue to stay negative. It is important to remember that people express themselves negatively for some reason; instead of confronting them, try to recognize the situation's usefulness and ask, sincerely, how staying stuck is helpful.

The second reason for including this excerpt is that when it is read—to either an individual or a group—it can direct a client's thoughts toward a better way of communicating with others, be they group members or the client's own family, spouse, children, employer, and friends. After reading the passage, the therapist can pose such questions to a client as the following:

Suppose you woke up tomorrow and were not wearing a synthetic smile, partaking in meaningless chatter, or feeling dull despair like the others around you, how would your family know this? Who would notice first? What difference would it make for you when that person noticed? What would that person notice about you that was different?

How would you assist your family in becoming more acquainted with their own individuality?

How would these new behaviors make a difference in your life?

Sometimes problems appear the most complicated when group clients truly believe that their problem will be solved only when someone else changes their behavior. (This is particularly true of a couples' group.) These group members may seem to count on such change in order to go on with their life and may perceive themselves as stuck until such change happens. Questions that are helpful in situations like this are the following:

What would it do for you when the behavior of —— changes?

Suppose that happened. What would you be doing on the day the change occurs that would be different from what you did yesterday?

Suppose —— never changes but you are ready to step back into life on a small scale. What behaviors would we all see, as we watched you go through your day, that would tell us you were getting back into life?

It is also helpful for the therapist to ask other members of the group to describe how they picture the member in question when that person gets back into life. Placing responsibility on the client who has a troubled relationship to focus on a future in which the other person does not change (and inviting group members to share their vision of the client in such a circumstance) brings reality home with a new twist: the client must imagine stepping into life again, even on a small scale, when the problem situation is still present (i.e., when the other person has made little or no change).

In other situations where clients are feeling overwhelmed by complicated problems, their beliefs seem to center around the need for a problem to be *totally* solved in order for their life to progress. By projecting out to a group the idea that small changes made in an effort to alleviate a problem can still improve the quality of one's life even when the problem is not completely removed, a therapist gives members a chance to brainstorm about how the life of an overwhelmed group member could be improved. The therapist may need to answer the "Yes, but . . ." responses of the client who views life as just too complicated by saying, "I understand how hard it is to envision this happening and how easy it is to imagine how it might not ever happen. But I'm still interested in what you would like to be doing instead."

The therapist and group members should support and praise the *smallest* action idea introduced by such a client, leaving the definition of the task to the client for the next week. The therapist can then ask group members to recall any actions on the part of the client during past group sessions that demonstrate the presence of the competencies the client now desires.

7. *Temporarily adopt each group member's worldview to lessen that client's resistance. Think of actions and behaviors as doing something important for the client, and attempt to assist the individual in the discovery of actions and behaviors that would be less dangerous and interfering than the ones currently used.*

Amy, a fourteen-year-old, was referred for counseling by her physician for school refusal. When she was confronted with a positive test for multiple illicit drugs, Amy admitted to drinking alcohol on a regular basis and to being sexually active with men in their twenties without using protection. Her mom also mentioned that each week Amy would leave home on Friday evening, travel to a large nearby city with friends (her mom had never met them), and then return on Sunday.

I met with Amy and Mom just before placing Amy in an adolescent girls' group. I assumed from Mom's hysterical phone call before our meeting that she wished for Amy to stop using drugs and to become more responsible for her life. Yet as we began our session, it appeared that both mother and daughter could not have cared less about the drug test results. Furthermore, Mom was convinced that Amy's behavior would not change. Frustrated, I tried to determine what they wanted from therapy.

LM: *What can we do in here today that would be productive for both of you?*

AMY: *Don't even think about telling me to stop using drugs. There's no way! I like using them, my friends all use them, and I have no intention of quitting.*

MOM: [Crying] *She just won't quit.*

LM: Amy, I have no intention of asking you to quit using drugs. I suppose they do something for you and while I am worried about your life, I will leave it up to you to tell me what you do want.

AMY: I want her [nodding at Mom] *to stop being so sad all the time. My dad is so mean to her. If they divorced, it would be fine with me. He roughs her up so much. Last week, he threw her up against the wall and hit me, too.*

LM: You sound so worried about your mom. You must love her very much.

AMY: [Beginning to cry] *I do.*

LM: Mom, since Dad isn't here today, I wonder what Amy could do that would help you to be less sad.

I silently hoped that I would hear Mom say something like "Give up using drugs" or "Stay at home more often" or "Tell me where she is going" or "Introduce me to her friends" or "Stop drinking." Something, *anything,* along those lines, but instead Mom replied: *"If she helped me with the dishes a few times during the week, I think I would feel better."*

LM: Okay, and what would that do for you?

MOM: We could spend time together, and maybe she would eat with her dad and me a couple of times per week in the evening.

LM: Sounds like you really miss your daughter.

MOM: I really do.

LM: Amy, what could your mom do to encourage you to do dishes and eat with your family two or three nights per week?

AMY: Stop yelling so much and crying all the time. We need to bring Dad in here next time.

LM: Good idea. Think you can try this for a week?

AMY: [Smiling] *I can do anything for a week.*

My personal beliefs about people's ability to find their way out of problems, given a cooperative context, were reaffirmed when Amy looked at me and said, "You know, I've been thinking about giving up drugs, actually. They really don't do anything for me anymore. I don't get high without taking lots and lots. My friends have even talked about quitting."

I replied, "Wow, sounds like a good idea for you. I trust you will do what you need to do."

Amy soon entered an adolescent girls' group, where her experiences were listened to eagerly by the members. As she gave up using drugs and spent more time with her mom, she seemed to take a new pride in herself; she was also able to offer good ideas to her fellow group members. I capitalized on Amy's ability to give up something that was important to her in exchange for a loving, warm, and respectful relationship with her mom.

Asking group members to discuss how their current behaviors offer comfort, relief, or gratification helps dissolve resistance. This is a helpful and resistance-stopping type of questioning that can be useful in groups focusing on violence, substance abuse, anger, or school issues. As group members identify with each other's experiences, the therapist can ask them for their ideas regarding more positive, less harmful (or less illegal) behaviors. This may begin a brainstorming session that leads in turn to exception identification. Such construction of alternative behaviors gives group clients an additional arsenal of strategies to try at various times.

8. *Help group members view their problem as* external *to themselves. This will help them see the problem as a separate entity that influences but does not always control their life.*

Consider the powerful message in the following exercise proposed to a group by the therapist: "For a few minutes, I would like you each to think of how the situation that is bothering you has influenced your life up to this moment. How has it influenced your relationships and your daily behaviors?" In this question the goal is to portray the problem as one that *bothers,* rather than *defines,* the individual. When Michael White wrote of externalizing problems, he offered the possibility of freedom to persons whose lives had been overtaken by a problem-saturated self-perception. By asking how the problem had been "affecting their lives and their relationships," White (1989, p. 5) helped them feel capable of intervening in their own lives.

Externalizing their situation can be a new way for members of specialized groups, such as those focusing on anger, depression, or loss, to manage their behaviors. Clients learn to think of their new actions as giant steps that move them away from their problem's influence on their life. To carry out this idea visually, group clients may be asked to personify their problem or to draw it using crayons, pencil, and paper. Children or adolescents may choose stuffed animals to represent their problem; as they hold the object, they can describe to the group the actions they take when the problem is influencing them. After such a description, clients can choose another object or stuffed animal that seems more comforting and that represents a solution or new action that will provide a better outcome. The therapist can then encourage group members to become a support team organized against their peer's externalized problem. At this point the therapist might ask group members to brainstorm additional ideas with their peer in an effort to develop solutions or actions based on strengths exhibited by the peer in group sessions or related to them in the peer's accounts of successful past experiences.

Consider the following dialogue, representative of the externalizing approach, that occurred between a family's members who were in a multifamily group setting:

> THERAPIST: *Just for a moment, I want you each to think of something very different regarding why you are here today. I want you to look at each other and think that no one in your family is a problem and, in fact, that the problem is that there is*

a problem interfering with your family's relationships. "It" may encourage arguments and result in hurt feelings, frustration, and a desire for revenge, and it is seriously crippling your relationships. As you think about it in this way, think of how you each nurture this problem and give it life in your home.

MOM: I yell too much, and then my husband interferes by taking the kid's side.

DAD: There's just so much tension between Mom and our older son. You could cut the tension with a knife, and I really get tired of being a referee.

SON: Yeah, but she nags me all the time about my homework, doing the yard work. I do have a life, you know.

THERAPIST: [To son] *Are there times when the tension is not there between you and Mom?*

SON: It seems like it happens every day.

THERAPIST: [To son] *This is a wild question, but I was wondering if there are ever any days when maybe you keep the tension out of the household?*

MOM: When he does what I need him to do.

SON: When you ask me and don't yell at me to do it, I usually do it. But most of the time you just yell.

THERAPIST: So when Mom asks you and doesn't yell at you, it's better. What else does she do on those days that gets your cooperation?

SON: She doesn't bug me to do it right away.

THERAPIST: How do you manage to get her to see you need some more time?

SON: I don't know.

MOM: He doesn't bark back at me. Instead, he tells me when he will do it, and I leave him alone.

DAD: They used to be really close when he was growing up. Since he's been in so many activities, the war has started. He just needs more time to do things than she's used to giving him.

THERAPIST: Mom, I know you supervise people at work. Have you ever worked with someone who was not quite as efficient as you?

MOM: All the time.

THERAPIST: Does tension try and intrude into your day?

MOM: All the time.

THERAPIST: Yet you say you've worked at the same place for ten years. How would you explain your ability to cope with tension at work so that it doesn't interfere with your job performance?

The dialogue reminds this family that the problem is an intruder that they have been able to avoid at certain times. By identifying their competencies and talking about times when the problem has *not* been an intruder, the therapist revives the family's confidence, which very often decreases conflict. As the group therapist listens for descriptions of problems, terms such as *it, the problem, this anger, the depression,* or *the situation* are identified as simple keywords that can be used to begin to talk about the problem as external, a technique that eliminates the need to blame others in the process. Keeping the problem external in the conversations is a relief because it gives participants an opportunity to see themselves as less problem-saturated.

In a group setting such as a multifamily group, listening to one family's members converse and identifying when the tension surfaces is educational for the other families and helps everyone see their own problems differently. The therapist can then ask observing group members, "As you listened to this family describe how they give in to the problem, what did you see or hear them do in their interactions with each other as they talked here today that increased the tension? What did they each do that seemed to avoid creating this tension?"

To the family the therapist might pose this question: "As a family, when you talked to me about avoiding the tension, were you thinking differently about yourselves?" And then the therapist might continue as follows: "Let's say that you leave today and, for only a week, you avoid the tension at all costs. What do you think you might each do differently, based on what you have told us here today, that would help this happen?

"Inviting persons to be an audience to their own performance of these alternative stories enhances the survival of the stories and the sense of personal agency," wrote White and Epston (1990, p. 17). Externalizing problems can give solution focused group therapists a simple way to talk about problems and help their group clients let go of pathological descriptions of themselves.

> 9. *Focus only on the possible and changeable. Assist group members in thinking more specifically and less emotionally when setting goals for therapy.*

When goal setting focuses on specific behaviors in group therapy, clients leave group sessions with new, measurable behaviors that help them redefine themselves whenever the problem arises and threatens to label them as incompetent. Whenever a group client states, "I just want to be happier," it is helpful for the therapist to ask, "When you are happier, someday, what would group members be seeing you do differently?" After a client describes what the new actions would be, the therapist should encourage group members to list additional behaviors that would also indicate that the client's happiness is occurring. If group members get off track and talk about the behaviors they do *not* want, the therapist can ask, "How would you like things to be for this member instead?"

Sometimes group clients are able to focus more on the possible and the changeable when their beliefs from the past about themselves are altered or reconstructed to fit who they want to be currently. For example, Susan, a member of a group for survivors of violence told me that prior to escaping from her violent husband to a shelter, she had viewed herself as worthless, stupid, and dependent. When I asked her to describe for the group how her life was before that relationship, she sat up straight and described her very successful career as a saleswoman in a car dealership. Before she married, she was independent and often had many male friends and suitors who desired her company. She described many of these men as successful at their jobs and kind and respectful toward her. She handled her horses after work and had a good relationship with her oldest son, who visited her often at her ranch. Her current description of the problem contrasted sharply with her true beliefs and actions from the past.

It was important at this point for Susan to receive support, validation, and encouragement. However, the group had difficulty in not talking about the reasons *why* she was depressed. Helping group members learn how to reinforce abilities of survivorship in each other can be accomplished by modeling and redirection from the therapist. To keep the group from commiserating with Susan, I made the following suggestions to them:

> What I think is remarkable is how Susan survived these awful events and still kept on trying to get herself back on track in spite of the difficulties. Her actual coming here today is an example of what I am talking about. (*Turning to the client*) I am impressed with your desire to reclaim your life and be the woman you want to truly be, because you have been there before. Your honesty with us and ability to tell us how you were successful in the past, despite the messages you received in your recent relationship, is remarkable. (*Turning to group*) What other strengths did you notice as Susan described her experience to us?

I then encouraged the group to discuss what things they thought Susan would be capable of doing in the near future when she, free from violence, began to live her former beliefs again. Their suggestions were very exciting for her to hear, giving her the emotional support she apparently needed. Before the session ended, Susan told the group that it was time for her to get her old job back and to begin making more money so that she would not "need a man" to survive. When Susan returned the next week, she was employed by a large cosmetic firm. When a group member asked what happened to the auto dealership job, she said, "I decided it was time to do what I have always wanted to do— sell perfume and cosmetics. I not only make a commission, I have an opportunity to move up in the company and *be someone* again."

If the group insists on talking about the problems a member has had and offers solutions that are obvious and that require the person to change, the therapist can redirect the group. For example, if members of Susan's group had approached her this way, I would have said something like this:

> Our conversation seems to be focusing on what's *wrong* with Susan. As I listen to all of you show such compassion and concern, I am wondering if this strategy is working so that Susan will know exactly what to do differently when she leaves here tonight. Before we end our group tonight, let's change the focus for a minute. Let's imagine that Susan returns next week having had a better week. What do all of you envision her doing that would tell you that she is doing things differently?

> *10. Go slowly and encourage group members to ease into solutions gradually. Help them see each new strategy as an experiment, not as a technique that guarantees success. Whatever happens as a result of a new strategy is simply part of an experiment toward change.*

When the therapist suggests limiting resolution of a problem to a brief time frame, clients often feel relieved that they are not required to make huge changes overnight. For example, when parents punish an adolescent by restricting a desired activity for the entire school year, they might well stifle any motivation on the teen's part to improve in order to lift the restriction. As an adolescent once reminded me, "When parents ground you forever, it doesn't give you any reason to get better. Instead, you just think, 'Well, I might as well misbehave again. How much worse can it get?' " The therapist who facilitates family groups or parenting groups should take note of this wisdom!

It is very helpful to encourage group members to attempt change gradually. Strongly caution them that lasting change takes time and practice. The solution focused group therapist may notice that clients who perceive their attempts to change behaviors as *practice* feel little stress and thus have a good opportunity to discover successful strategies. This caution to take things slow is particularly important when working with adolescents in groups, because often the words of caution instigate a paradoxical intervention. So be it!

An effective method of measuring small amounts of success efficiently is one that suggests a need for change on the basis of a person's position on a scale. For example, a therapist facilitating a women's relationship group might try getting the group on a new track after their initial introductions by saying: "Suppose I gave you a scale from one to ten. A ten means you or your partner always put all of your energy into making the relationship work. A one means you or your partner never put any energy into making the relationship work. Where are you on this scale? Where is your partner?"

Using the scaling question can be enlightening to a group, for it asks members to share with others an account of their attempts at making a relationship work and thus allows each member to identify with others who may be doing too much or too little. The therapist can continue the exercise by asking a member, "When you compare your position on the scale with your partner's position, what seems to be a logical step for you to take for just a week?" The therapist can then ask the other group members what they think this individual needs to do to readjust her scale so that it seems more balanced. This type of conversation is supportive not only to those persons who expect others to change first but also to those who do too much or try too hard in a relationship. By offering a logical explanation of why they are stuck, it encourages them to take a much-needed break from giving.

NEW THOUGHTS ON OLD IDEAS: GIVING TRADITIONAL GROUPS A NEW FOCUS

You're never too old to become younger.

—Mae West

Throughout this book I provide clear ideas for developing specific questions that fit specific situations so that you, the reader, will grasp the concept of focusing on exception behaviors and solutions rather than problems. My purpose in giving such specific examples is to help you recognize what your group members need to do or think about to become solution focused within the group process. Remind yourself often that while the questions are solution focused, it is your thinking that is as important as any question you ask during a group session. It is your perseverance with "solution talk"—directing group members toward a collaborative conversation of strengths and abilities while cooperating with their need to talk about their problems—that is your greatest challenge. The following case is a good example of how a group and its social worker underwent such a process.

Sue, a determined and creative social worker who facilitated family-of-origin groups in a psychiatric inpatient facility, invited me to consult at one of her group sessions. On the chalkboard she had drawn a genogram for one of the group members. Sue confided to me how hard it had been trying to change the focus of the group and to keep group members from commiserating with each other over past family issues. She was in the process of learning solution focused ideas herself and was excited about the prospect of integrating them in her group. However, the group, used to a more traditional analytical style, kept responding to her solution focused questions with "I don't know" or "I don't think anything good will ever happen." It seemed as if their diagnoses had taken such a prominent place in their lives that they had little idea of how to possibly see anything other than what was causing them pain in their lives.

Sue's challenge was to help group members move forward with confidence, to steer them in a solution focused direction while still respecting their need to talk about why they were in treatment. Most of her group members, such as those who were court-mandated to attend sessions and those who were suspended from their jobs, felt robbed of self-confidence. Most members were ready to blame their extended families for their deficits and mistakes; while a few took responsibility for the present, they still blamed their families for their low self-esteem. Sue hoped to assist group members in looking at their family systems, the source, they claimed, of abuse, anger, and resentment, and finding even a small trace of family strength to grasp. She was hopeful that this would help them see themselves differently. The following dialogue was exchanged during my visit:

THERAPIST: Looking at Al's family history, what family members do you see in the genogram who did not have a drug or alcohol problem?

GROUP MEMBER 1: There are quite a few on his father's side. Looks like most of the drinkers were on the mother's side.

AL: Most of the people who did drugs or drank were on my mother's side. She smoked marijuana with me when I was younger. Her brother bought me beer when I was in high school.

THERAPIST: I wonder what it was about your father's side of the family that kept them from using drugs or drinking. What were their strengths?

AL: They were all into work. They were workaholics.

THERAPIST: You know, you seem to have a pretty good job. Your boss sent you here and he's promising to put you back in your old position when you're discharged. I wonder what that says about you. What do the rest of you think it says for him?

GROUP MEMBER 3: He works hard here on the unit! He's supported me when I was really down. I keep telling him to take care of himself, not everybody else!

GROUP MEMBER 2: Yeah, he's sort of the one people go to when they want a friend. He's been very helpful to me.

GROUP MEMBER 4: I think he really wants to quit. He's always ready to go to the AA meeting, and he tries so hard to talk to his wife about how he wants things different with her and the kids.

THERAPIST: Who was it in your family, on your father's side, who seemed to believe in families the way you do?

AL: My dad. He tried. It was just that my mom was always drunk and screaming. He eventually just stayed at work.

THERAPIST: I wonder what will happen when you begin using some of the traits on your father's side to keep on staying straight?

AL: I'll probably work more and come home instead of taking off after lunch to drink.

The dialogues presented in this chapter served as the beginning of solution focused groups within several psychiatric settings. During the training, the staff and I noticed how clients changed their perceptions of themselves from damaged goods to survivors. As some groups became more and more solution focused while others stayed problem focused, which was a typical problem I encountered when I entered the facilities, clients' group preferences began to be a cause of concern for the case managers. Clients were choosing the solution focused groups because they found them to be more uplifting and positive. The clients in those groups appeared more animated, were more positive, and seemed to take action to change their relationships and their life goals more frequently. Many of these clients commented that they appreciated not being asked about the details of their problems, since they had repeated those details so many times to so many people in the treatment setting. People in solution focused groups simply got happier sooner.

CONCLUSION

This chapter offers some basic ideas and assumptions of solution focused therapy and describes its application in the group therapy situation. This book offers therapists new ways of inviting clients to join a unique club—one in which the context is that of *discovery* rather than *pathology*. In the dialogues presented in this book, the reader is given the opportunity to listen to the stories brought by group members as they begin practicing the search for *exceptions* in their lives. This model gives group therapists many new assistants to help them look for exceptions in the behaviors of their own clients and guide them in a new direction.

The following chapters contain ideas for groups in specific situations and with specific needs. All descriptions of groups and therapists in these chapters reflect a solution focus. Notice how questions from individual therapy sessions evolve into group therapy questions and help the therapist integrate the client into the group setting, thus adding a new set of eyes to observe the group process.

2 Beginning the Group Process with a New Conversation

Solitude is fine, but you need someone to tell you that solitude is fine.

—Honoré de Balzac

Maslow (1968) has called the four lower level needs for survival, safety, belonging and self-esteem deficiency needs. . . . When these needs are more or less satisfied, we turn to the higher level needs for intellectual achievement, aesthetic appreciation and finally, self-actualization" (Woolfolk, 1995, pp. 348–49). Whether we group together as preschoolers to play in the sandbox or meet with friends at the junior high dance or later in life congregate at a senior citizen picnic, belonging to a group seems to bring us a sense of importance, acceptance, support, and validity in our lives—something we can't always achieve on our own. When individuals enter group therapy with a solution focused brief therapist, they soon learn that the session is different from traditional therapy because the focus is on abilities, not deficits. The relationship between therapist and client becomes one of partners engaged in discovery. Clients may leave therapy sessions priding themselves on accomplishments of theirs that were mentioned during the session by the therapist. I recall a client who once replied to my question of "What did we do in here today that might have made a difference?" with the following answer: "I'm not sure. I only know that because we talked today, I can leave here thinking that things are not as bad as I thought."

Imagine that thought held by six or more people instead of just one. Imagine clients having a place to go every other week where they know there is an oasis of support waiting for them. Sounds encouraging and appealing, doesn't it? Yet getting clients to enter group therapy can be a challenge. Managed health care plans are designed to contain the costs of mental health services, and they challenge the therapist to do so while delivering effective treatment. Fewer therapy visits, not quality of therapy visits, seems to be the underlying message heard by therapists as they plead with precertification specialists regarding the numbers of allowable visits. Given this situation, group therapy enables therapists to offer attractive treatment alternatives for consideration by managed care companies. Tracy Todd, Ph.D., an expert who works with therapy practices and collaborates with managed care companies says that managed care companies are constantly trying to find good quality therapy practices and that those practitioners who have planned group therapy sessions may have an advantage. He also gives the following good advice to therapists who are interested in beginning groups:

> A common mistake made by clinicians, when asked by managed care systems if they practice group therapy, is the response that they are willing to run a group, but they are unable to produce a start date or target population. It is amazing how many providers are "about to" start a group but cannot produce dates, times or topics. If you feel comfortable running a group, be specific about it to the managed care system. Two suggestions may be helpful. First, develop a flyer advertising the group. Clinicians in the managed care system can copy it, discuss it with clients in their office, and, it is hoped, answer questions clients may ask. Second, run a time-limited group. A time-limited group demonstrates that you have a specific agenda for clients; the managed care system will not be as concerned as with a support group that goes on indefinitely. (Todd, 1994, p. 31)

In private practice I often perform assessments of employees for large companies. This initial assessment can be conducted as an individual therapy session, particularly when utilizing the Admission Interview for Group Therapy (found later in this chapter). (Todd suggests that a therapist desiring to develop a more lucrative practice should consider having time-limited groups, meeting for approximately six sessions, for men, women, adolescents, parents, or couples. Todd has suggested that in the case of capitation plans one's co-pay multiplied by five or six clients makes for a profitable hour of therapy for everyone.) After the client has been assessed or has visited with the therapist for the first session, the therapist may offer the option of group therapy to suitable clients. For example, to a candidate for a women's group the therapist might say:

> I have a group for women that I have recently started here in my office, and I think your ideas and comments would make a nice contribution to our conversations. Your goals seem to have so much in common with the goals that many of the women share. You know where you are going and you are determined to get there. We meet every other week for one hour and a half on Wednesday evenings at six. The next time we meet is June 6.

This invitation suggests that the therapist believes the client is progressing. Moreover, by *not* keeping her in individual therapy, the therapist also conveys the message that the client is competent.

In the case of adolescents who do not want to attend group, ask them just to visit once. Talk to them about the competencies you discovered about them during individual therapy and how helpful you perceive their being in a group setting with other teens would be. Typically, adolescents in group therapy bond easily, especially if group members hear the following message from the therapist:

> I'm on your side. I'm for getting you out of this group as soon as possible so you can prove to your parents [or parole officer, school principal, teachers] that they have misjudged your abilities. To do that, we have to change your reputations so that they see who you really are on the inside. Let's talk about what they need to begin seeing in you so that they start backing off.

The idea that the therapist is on the side of the adolescent clients lessens their resistance, puts the adolescents in charge of their own solutions, and opens up better opportunities for dialogue between group members, since the adult therapist is asking them for their thoughts instead of trying to preach to them. Especially in the adolescent group setting, where group members have come to therapy after having done something to offend some adult in their lives, such an opportunity to clear the air and express themselves is welcomed. Confrontation alienates teens whereas asking for their own input brings them closer to being honest with themselves about what is needed to change their lives. This warm context, along with the therapist's desire to truly understand each teen's problem, will validate and signal acceptance of each adolescent into the group and will encourage more of the same by other members.

THE ROLE OF THE SOLUTION FOCUSED GROUP FACILITATOR (*AKA TOUR GUIDE*)

You can tell more about a person by what he says about others than you can by what others say about him.

—Leo Aikman

As the introductory paragraphs of this chapter make clear, in order to facilitate groups with a solution focus it is important for the therapist to believe that group members are capable, competent people who can resolve their difficulties. What are your own views about how people change? Do group members need you to come up with strategies to enable them to walk out of the group session competent? Do you see yourself as a necessary link between problem resolution and success for your group clients? Your opinions can keep you solution focused or hinder your progress in developing a solution focused group. It is therefore helpful to stop and consider your personal views of how people change their lives and what *you* think they need to do to solve their problems. Take a few moments to fill out the following worksheet. Lines are provided for note taking and examples.

If you agreed with most of these statements, you truly are aware of the abilities and competencies of clients. If you disagreed with some,

MY PERCEPTIONS OF HOW CHANGE HAPPENS

1. *Given a cooperative context, clients are capable of solving their own problems.*

   _____

   _____

2. *Clients can create or discourage situations in which problems occur.*

   _____

   _____

3. *Clients feel more competent when they design their own strategies to solve problems.*

   _____

   _____

4. *When a client seems resistant, the therapist should change strategies.*

   _____

   _____

5. *Problems do not cripple clients; clients' perception of their problem cripples them.*

   _____

   _____

6. *Reflecting competency in a group seeds the unconscious for later actions.*

   _____

   _____

7. *Symptoms are problems that clients are unable to articulate and, instead, act on.*

    _____

    _____

8. *Problem "dis-solving" is a collaborative process during which clients remember times when problems happened less frequently.*

    _____

    _____

perhaps your ideas about how change happens will be challenged. Having some reservations about the statements is a common response to solution focused ideas. The best way to work with this is to accept that you have different views because of your personality, experience, education, and the way that you have possibly worked through situations in your own life. Be cautious that your experiences don't get in the way of your clients' abilities and keep you from recognizing new solutions.

Think also about the clients you are currently seeing in individual therapy or in a group setting. Look over your case notes and examine them closely for ideas that indicate how change occurred or is still occurring in your clients' lives. What did you do, if anything, that made a difference? (Ask them!) What did they do? What types of questions did they respond to? How did you cooperate with them to keep them in therapy? Ask yourself, "What would my *clients* say I did that made a difference?" (See Metcalf & Thomas, 1994.) I make it a point to always ask my clients at the end of a therapy session, "What did we do in here today that might have made a difference for you?" I tell my clients that I ask this question because I am interested in what *they* think is making a difference, if any, in our sessions. After all, I want to do more of what works and less of what has not worked.

KEEPING THE GROUP ON THE SOLUTION TRACK

Within the solution focused circle of therapists, there is a basic belief that people are competent and, given an atmosphere where they can experience such competency, are able to solve their own problems. This atmosphere is of utmost importance in the group situation, where members tend to jump in and give each other advice. Facilitators might consider thinking of themselves not as a leader but as a sort of tour guide, co-discoverer, or co-constructor of solutions. When facilitators take on more prominent roles, clients have less chance of seeing themselves as competent. If you have ever led a group where you felt that you did all of the work and needed to do even more for the group to work, ask yourself the following questions:

On a scale of 1 to 10, with 1 meaning I did nothing and 10 meaning I did everything, where was I when the group ended?

Where was the group as a whole?

If you found yourself near the 10 mark and the group at a lower mark, you might have been doing too much. As is true in couples' therapy and of clients in group therapy, those who take on more prominent roles hinder those who are not as conspicuous. Therefore, a slight adjustment of activity on the therapist's part can instigate more activity on the part of the group members. This slight adjustment may mean saying to a group, "I am stumped. I am without any solution for you. What do you think you will need to do to begin changing things on your own?" The therapist might then specifically ask the group to identify those behaviors used in the past by the member under discussion that might help solve that member's current problem.

The therapist who enjoys suggesting strategies for clients may need to learn that silence is a powerful tool while facilitating a solution focused group. Instead, the therapist needs to wait to suggest ideas of competence until they emerge from the conversations at hand and needs to make sure the direction is toward exception building. This is a difficult task, because group members typically will tell their stories when they hear other stories that are similar to their own. This commiseration bonds people together yet keeps them stuck. It is better for the therapist to use the strategy of silence during this time and take notes about the group members who are talking. Ideas to consider while watching and listening are as follows:

What strengths or skills is this person using to talk in group today?

What are some of the probable abilities that this person uses on the job that might help in resolving this problem?

Has this person been in relationships long? How might diligence and patience help this person today in thinking of new solutions?

How does this group member, who has such a chaotic life, find time to make it to group? What might this say about this person's priorities?

How does this member relate to others in the group? How might these traits translate to the person's home life?

What does helping the other adolescents in the group do for this supposedly angry and rebellious adolescent? How might having the opportunity at home to do the same make a difference?

Taking a back seat in group to watch group members step out of their pathology means *watching for exception behaviors at that moment and at every moment!* Consider adopting the following strategies before your next group session:

Watch group members differently.

Write down at least three things about each group member that shows that person's strengths.

Pretend that your job is only to observe members' strengths, as if your clients are moving out of their problems for the next hour.

Share with group members all of your observations before the group ends. Think of writing down the strengths of each member in such a way that you can easily make photocopies of your remarks. Your clients will want them! Let them know that the strengths you have noticed about them might be helpful to them during the next week or so. They will appreciate your efforts. Brian Cade often remarks that it is impossible for therapists to not influence their clients. Your remarks about a client's abilities come from your observations, something that all clients value (or else they would not be attending). Your credibility will go on the line to further your clients' abilities outside of group. Watch for change during the next group session and begin the session by asking, "What's been different since we last met?"

SOLUTION FOCUSED IDEAS TO CONSIDER

The best way to keep groups moving toward solutions is to learn how to stay on *their* track, toward *their* goals, using *their* skills and abilities. If the group therapist recognizes and works with the clients' needs, expectations, problem behaviors, and competencies, then further cooperation will develop in the client, resulting in a client–therapist relationship that models effective interaction for all the group members. Clients are more likely to continue coming to group therapy and to attempt the tasks that develop through therapy when the therapist approaches them in a familiar, cooperative, respectful, and nonconfronting manner. The following questions may serve as a way for therapists to reexamine their track of therapy when they feel frustrated by a seeming lack of progress with a group. These questions can be asked silently by the therapist or directly to the group, depending on the situation.

 1. *What do clients hope to achieve during group therapy (i.e.,*
     as revealed in the admission interview)?

Asking this simple question starts off the solution focused group process by placing the group clients in charge of information gathering. When I begin groups, I tell my clients that I am interested in learning only what they think I need to know about them. I tell them that I trust that they will tell me all I need to know without my guessing or hypothesizing. For many, this is a relief. For the small percentage who do want to tell me more, I respect that need, listen closely, and encourage group members to listen for strengths as the story is told. The importance of staying focused only on what the client brings to group therapy makes the goals clear and solvable and keeps group members focused on issues they can control.

For example, the adolescent who attends group after running away from home may tell me that his parents made him come to group without his consent; in other words, he was sent. The adult on probation will tell me that his probation officer wants to hear that he is improving so that he will not need to see him as often. The family with a daughter dealing with anorexia will probably tell me that they want their daughter to be healthy. Hearing clients' requests for therapy and putting aside my own ideas and hypotheses will enlist them in the therapy process more easily and assist me in getting them to their desired goals. It has also been my experience that working in this way allows side issues to surface when they are appropriate and that these are more readily resolved when the main issue of concern is dissolving.

> 2. *What are the clues about how clients function in life, as indicated by the way they speak in group sessions regarding their strategies for conducting relationships with family members, friends, bosses, etc.? How do clients approach other group members and respond to other situations of concern?*

People are more effective in finding solutions to problems in their lives than they realize. When life becomes a burden, they tend to notice other burdens more easily and fail to recognize their past successes. The successful supervisor who has difficulties communicating at home may not recognize his own skill level in relationships at work. The person dealing with an alcohol problem may not realize how much she disciplines herself at work. The woman who binges at home yet never binges at work for fear of getting off track with her assignments might need to notice how a structured and organized job environment discourages out-of-control eating. A client's concern for family members, a tendency to schedule and keep appointments on time, a gracious manner in accepting compliments in therapy, good listening skills while conversing with friends and family members—all are strengths the therapist must recognize and eventually make the client aware of.

I worked recently with a women's group in which there was a client who would have been diagnosed several years ago as her daughter's "co-dependent," a then-popular pathological label. As June told me of the countless times she bailed her daughter out of jail and paid her daughter's overdue bills and legal fees, I thought of the many ways that she was trying harder than her daughter to be responsible. The group pounced upon her at one point, saying that she was working too hard to help her daughter and that she needed to quit. June withdrew and did not speak unless it was to defend herself. Noticing her dilemma, I presented a scaling question to her and to the group for consideration, a question with which the group readily assisted her.

> *LM: On a scale of 1 to 10, with a 1 meaning you are not doing anything to help your daughter to be responsible for her own life and actions* [this client's goal] *and 10 meaning you are doing everything you can for her, where would you say you are?*
>
> *CLIENT: A 10.*
>
> *LM: Where would you say your daughter is?*
>
> *CLIENT: About a 3.*
>
> *GROUP MEMBER: She's a minus 5.*

The more June talked about what she had done to help her daughter become more responsible, the more the group discouraged her overcommitment. First, I redescribed her behaviors as very helpful attempts to help her daughter take responsibility for herself. I then wrote down her attempts as "strategies" for assisting her daughter to become responsible. After recording fifteen strategies, I went back through each of them and asked June to tell me which ones were successful with her daughter. I checked only three that were effective and, with her approval, crossed out the twelve others. As we ended our session, I asked June to consider using only those three strategies for the next two weeks. She agreed that there was no reason to do what didn't work. The remaining three strategies were as follows:

> Spend quality time with my daughter as an adult companion (e.g., going to the movies together).
>
> Talk to her about how important family life is.
>
> Help her see herself as worthy (e.g., help her pick out clothing that accents a positive self-image).

All these strategies are kind, warm, and concerned behaviors of a mother who was trying to launch her child into adulthood. They are also closely related to who June was in her professional life—a medical secretary who answered the phone calls of distraught patients and concerned parents so efficiently that she had been employed by the same pediatrician for ten years. June's other twelve strategies involved her being more responsible for her daughter's issues than her daughter was. Recognizing her own strengths and what she wanted to do for her daughter, June remained true to her personality and was able to eliminate those strategies for teaching her daughter to be a responsible adult that had proven ineffective.

3. *What would group clients like the significant others in their lives to know about them? How would that new knowledge be beneficial to the clients?*

This is a resistance-busting question for therapists who work with adolescents and children. By suggesting to adolescents that they need to change their reputation, a technique that a new self-awareness on the part of the teen and a desire to prove the adults' impressions wrong replaces problematic behavior. This clever means of cooperating successfully lessens resistance and models how an adult can effectively relate to adolescents. When the therapist then speaks differently of the adolescent to parents and shares such an idea, family collaboration happens more easily. The family is then asked to observe any change in behavior on the part of the adolescent.

By asking the family to watch for more positive behaviors as a "group," the skills inherent in solution focused group therapy work for the family in family therapy. For example, when an adolescent lives in a blended family and travels from one stepfamily to the other on weekends or during visitation, I often invite both sets of parents to a group meeting with the adolescent so that everyone is on the same page in cooperating with each other and expecting the same behavior from the adolescent. Working first with the sets of parents and giving the adolescent what I refer to as a "well-deserved rest" in the waiting room, I encourage the adults to discuss what they want for the child. Then, after discussing current strategies and deciding on which ones have worked previously, we come up with a plan that enhances the attributes of the adolescent.

In one case, a sixteen-year-old girl, Alison, was caught in a sexual situation in a car with her boyfriend after sneaking out of the house at three in the morning. The parents and stepparents had different ideas about how to handle the situation, although both sets of parents were concerned about the girl's well-being. To begin the session, I asked everyone in the room, including Alison, to state their concerns. Here is my tally of the results:

- The father wanted to forbid his daughter to see the boyfriend. He was extremely opposed to placing her on birth-control pills, saying that giving them to her was like giving her permission to have sex.
- The mother wanted to place her daughter on birth-control pills.
- The stepfather feared that restricting contact with the boyfriend would cause rebellion and suggested that they allow the girl to go out with him within strict limits and to make her own decisions regarding her sexual behavior.
- The stepmother wanted more restrictions and consequences, similar to what she used in raising her own teenage son, who was very successful in school.
- Alison was very quiet, yet she did tell everyone that she knew she had lost their trust and that she wanted to regain it by proving that she could be responsible and follow rules.

All of these ideas were developed out of love and concern, but Alison was caught in a web of too many opinions. She had acted on her own initiative to see her boyfriend, regardless of the possible consequences, since the rules were different at each household. Focusing on her negative behavior would have created an environment where blame and guilt could develop, and reprimanding her probably would have pushed her into more rebellion. Alison appeared to me to be a competent, successful adolescent (she held a part-time job after school and was making good grades).

I asked all of the parents to describe Alison's strengths and assets. Then, giving them credit for knowing her better than I ever would, I asked them for their own strategies for talking and working out problems with her in the past. There was much discussion, and everyone agreed that a sensitive, kind, yet concerned approach would have the best impact, since Alison was often rather inhibited and shy when confronted with issues. After everyone voiced their concerns, I asked them to tell me what their goals were for Alison. They replied in consensus on the following:

- Keep her from becoming pregnant or infected with sexually transmitted diseases.
- Restore her self-confidence and help her to believe that she should be respected by young men.
- Help her respect and follow through with family rules.
- Help her make good decisions about her choices in boyfriends.

These goals made sense to everyone. My role was to gather the information and translate the goals into statements that everyone agreed upon. The boyfriend, according to all of the parents, had been in jail and was often in gang-related fights. Their concerns about Alison's association with him were valid, yet, as I later learned when I interviewed her, Alison had affection for him and wished to continue their relationship. Her statements during the interview *("I want to continue seeing him until I realize that he is not good for me. He's changed, he really has.")* told me that contact with him would be inevitable and that her family's attempts to separate them would be fruitless. With Alison determined to learn for herself who her boyfriend was and with her parents and stepparents just as determined to help her make that decision, my role was to combine and blend both intentions collaboratively. With Alison's permission, I shared her desire with her parents and stepparents. I acknowledged that their worries about the safety of their daughter were valid, but I pointed out that her desire to choose and be with a companion were valid also. I read the list of goals back to the family. Then, parents, stepparents, and daughter came up with the following strategies:

- Alison can see the boyfriend only when supervised at either household. (She was told by everyone that they wanted to learn to trust him and appreciate his qualities as she did but could only do this by seeing him often and in a supervised situation.)
- Alison is to expand her circle of friends and to date others. (Alison readily agreed to this. Her parents told her that she was beautiful and that many young men deserved an opportunity to see in her what her parents and stepparents all saw in her.)
- Alison is to be accompanied by her mother to a gynecologist for an exam and for a discussion of methods of birth control and protection against sexually transmitted diseases. (This was to happen as soon as possible.)
- Alison and her father are to have an open discussion about the appropriate time to engage in sex. (While the father felt slightly uncomfortable about this, he realized through the discussion that it was indeed important to have this talk with his daughter in order to achieve the goals described.)

The stepparents agreed to support their spouses and reassured Alison that they loved her and were behind her 100 percent in helping her regain her self-respect.

This example indicates how a group therapy format can facilitate a collaborative process with a family while respecting the needs and wishes of family members and client. By asking for the goals each adult had for their daughter, I helped them identify desired outcomes. On the basis of positive past experiences with their daughter, the parents were then able to develop workable strategies. (Six months later Alison changed boyfriends and chose not to go on birth control, because she realized that sex at her age was too risky. She finished high school, and her father reported that her self-image had greatly improved. He also said that he and his wife realized through this situation how important having similar rules and constant communication at both households had been for their daughter's well-being.)

4. *What past successes in solving previous difficult problems have the clients had? How do they explain their past successes?*

In a group setting it is always interesting to hear relationship dilemmas brought up by clients who view themselves as ineffective communicators yet are able to deliver their message to the other group members without difficulty. The child who participates in an "anger management" group appropriately and without acting out is telling the therapist something about his abilities to control anger. The shy child who speaks to an individual therapist yet isolates herself in a group for relationship building in elementary school probably needs to be left alone until she is ready to speak. The woman who offers too much advice to the other women in her support group might find it helpful to first be told by the therapist that advice giving seems to be very important to her and then asked, "When is it that you find others most receptive to you?" Listen and watch for behaviors that are characteristic of the person. These can be quite obvious during a group process. Recognizing them and promoting clients' awareness of them can help clients in other areas of life.

5. *What are the goals and dreams of the clients? What does this say about priorities, needs, and personhood? What is obvious in group interactions regarding their interpersonal strengths with others?*

The miracle question is a vehicle to use with a group to move them past a problem focus and into the future, fantasizing all the way. "The framework of the miracle question and other questions of this type allows clients to bypass their structural, causal assumptions" (de Shazer, 1991, p. 113). People need dreams to hold on to when life becomes too difficult. The dreams of clients can tell us much about where they want to go in life, dreams they are afraid to pursue because of problems getting in their way. Challenging clients to dream while they are feeling stuck on a traumatic event, such as an incident of sexual abuse, can be accomplished by saying:

Dream with me for a minute. Suppose tomorrow morning you woke up and this event that has troubled you was less influential in your life. How would you know? How would others know? What would others see you doing differently? Think about the issues you brought to talk about in group today. What regrets would you have five years from now if you stayed stuck with your current issue versus taking a risk and doing what you sometimes dream about? What rewards would you imagine having if you took the risk and it worked out? How would you begin doing this on a very small scale, just for the next week, so that the chances of having regrets five years from now are less?

Watch clients closely as this exercise proceeds. The demeanor of the group often changes from sullen to hopeful when this exercise is performed, since the idea of being stuck in regrets is about as unattractive to people as the event that burdened them in the first place. Assisting group clients to imagine life without the problem gives them temporary relief from the intrusiveness of the traumatic event, and when clients feel freer emotionally, new behaviors are more likely.

6. *How quickly and efficiently do clients perform the tasks discussed in therapy? How agreeable are they to suggestions made by other group members or the therapist?*

My personal rule in group therapy (as well as individual therapy) is this: If the client is not following through on strategies developed during sessions, I am not on the same track as the client and I need to change direction. In the group situation, I may also need to redirect other group members from trying to force change in an individual; I do so by modeling cooperation with the client who is holding on to old behaviors and showing respect for that person's needs. The therapist might approach such a member by saying, "I've noticed that the ideas we discussed in group last time did not seem to work out for you. Apparently, we're missing something. Can you tell us what we need to know about working with you so that together we can come up with ideas that make more sense to you?"

In therapy groups the tendency may be for members to commiserate with each other because they believe they cannot move forward. Perhaps it is due to being given a diagnosis previously or to explanations from other therapists whose strategy was to promote insight. Whatever the reason a client feels stuck in an old story, it is still appropriate to ask if talking about the problem over and over again is producing new life strategies. There is less tendency for group commiseration to occur when members are asked for strategies from the beginning of the group's existence and the therapist refrains from suggesting them.

7. *What have others (other therapists or ministers, friends, or family members) tried that have helped or hindered a group client's progress toward solutions?*

When people are court-ordered to attend groups, they are participating in a process they often have little desire to invest in beyond pleasing the person in charge. Check out what might be occurring with such clients and ask their opinion of what has been done in the past that was even slightly helpful. Additionally, ask them to describe what was tried in an effort to assist them and what methods resulted in a behavior change that benefited them. A therapist needs to know the individual needs of group clients, and this inquiry will help to accomplish that. A question to ask at the end of a group session is this: "What have we done in here today that you have found helpful, if anything?" The therapist can elaborate on this question as follows: "I'm interested in doing what seems to work for all of you. Can you each tell me what we've done so far that has made a difference? What have some of your group members done that has been helpful to you? Suppose this group ends next week and you are interviewed by people who need to know how it benefited you. What would you imagine saying to them?"

Again, the purpose of these questions is to cooperate with the needs and goals of each group member and to suggest that group members are competent. The therapist can then simply listen, his role being that of facilitator, not leader. The therapist can then facilitate the therapeutic process by introducing those items that fit and mesh with the needs of the group clients.

A final question is one for therapists to consider privately: Given the answers from the above questions, what is the best way to cooperate and work with each client in the present situation? When a group session ends, it is time to gather one's thoughts from the group process and consider the clients as individuals with their own unique needs, desires, dreams, and personalities. This exercise can help the therapist approach the next group session with a clearer vision. If there is a feeling of frustration when reviewing a group's progress, a therapist might consider the following questions:

What am I pushing for that group members are *not* pushing for?

What is it that individual group members are trying to tell me through their actions and responses that they are not willing to do?

THE ADMISSION INTERVIEW FOR GROUP THERAPY

The questions provided below will be helpful for therapists to use when determining the needs of clients entering group therapy. The admission interview is to be completed by client and therapist during an individual assessment session. Completion of the interview certifies that the decision to attend group therapy is a reflection of the client's perception that he or she wants, needs, and is expected to do things differently in life. In conducting the admission interview, the therapist refers to the client's reason for seeking help as "the problem" and refers to it as if it were external to the person of the client. The problem is regarded as something that interferes in the life of the client, and the client as someone who has allowed that interference. The treatment setting is then described as a context in which the client can learn to avoid the interference of the problem by new behaviors, thoughts, and beliefs.

ADMISSION INTERVIEW

1. *Tell me what you think I need to know about the problem that has brought you here today. I am interested in your ideas. [If the client says that therapy was someone else's idea, ask: "What would that person probably say was their reason for asking you to be here?"]*

    _____

    _____

    _____

2. *When you look back, when was it that the problem did not affect you as much as it does now? What went on then that was different from now? What did you do then that made things different? What did others do?*

    _____

    _____

    _____

3. *When you have completed our group therapy program, what will you be doing differently that will assure you and your close significant others that you are ready to leave? [Ask the client for specific overt behaviors. If the client says, "I will be less angry," ask, "How will others know that? Who specifically will notice first?"]*

    _____

    _____

    _____

4. *Ask about how other people at work and in other important relationships know that the client's life is on track. [Probation officers, Employers]*

    _____

    _____

    _____

5. *In terms of the answers you gave for the two previous questions, how would you state your goal for your group therapy experience?*

    _____

    _____

    _____

6. *On the scale below, where are you currently in achieving your stated goal? [This scaling question is for the purpose of planning group selection and understanding where the client views current goal achievement.]*

    Problem is in control of me   I am in control of problem

    _____

    1   2   3   4   5   6   7   8   9   10

7. *In reference to your group therapy options, which of the following groups seem the most helpful for you to attend while in treatment?*

    _____ Multifamily Therapy

    _____ Chemical Management Group

    _____ Experiential Group Therapy

    _____ Anger Group

    _____ A.M./P.M. Process Group (for inpatient or daypatient programs)

    _____ Adolescent Process Group

    _____ Relationship Group (couples)

    _____ Women's Issues

    _____ Men's Issues

    _____ Survivor's Group (sexual abuse)

    _____ Eating Issues (eating disorders)

    _____ Parenting Skills

    _____ Children's Process Group

    _____

    assessment person

    _____

    client signature

FACILITATING THE GROUP PROCESS

THE FIRST GROUP MEETING

Here are specific suggestions for techniques therapists can use when clients meet for their first group session:

1. Set the mood for focusing on solutions.

After welcoming clients to the group, say, "As you introduce yourself, give us a brief idea as to why you are here and tell us what you think we should know." If a client was sent for group therapy (by a parent, spouse, parole officer, therapist, or employer), ask the client what that person would probably say he or she needs to see the client doing differently to warrant terminating therapy.

2. Suggest goal setting.

Encourage each client to identify a specific therapeutic goal by asking, "What will be going on in the future that will tell you and each of us that things are better for you?" If the person describes what others will be doing and forgets to focus on his or her own goal or behavior, help by asking specific questions such as, "What will *you* be doing in that picture?"

3. Search for exceptions to clients' problems.

Briefly acknowledge clients' struggles with their problem and express respect for their decision to seek therapy. Then direct their attention to what life was like before the problem appeared:

I've been listening to you talk about the reasons you are here today. Your situations sound quite challenging, and I admire you all for coming here to make things better in your life.

　　Just for a change of pace, let's talk about those times before the problem started to interfere in your life and what you were doing then that kept it away. How did you do that? Where were you? Who was there? How did that keep the problem smaller and not as intrusive? What were you believing about yourself when you were acting differently and the problem was not as predominant?

I wonder what might occur if, for just a day or even a few days, you believed in yourself like you did back then? Tell us what you would each be doing on those days.

4. Encourage motivation.

The therapist can help maintain clients' motivation by periodically posing such questions as the following:

Someday, when the problem that brought you here to group is less of a problem in your life, what will you get to do more of?

As you listen to your peers, is there someone in our group whom you might like to encourage to do something different?

As we talked today, who noticed a peer who "gave up" a problem and appeared to be more problem free during our conversations?

The therapist might ask a group member who appears free of a problem during the current session, "How is it that you were able to do this today?"

5. Assist group members with task development.

When individual clients' goals have been identified, the therapist can encourage clients to work toward their goals between therapy sessions: "You have all told me some great ideas by describing to me the times when the problem bothers you less. Let's now talk about what you think you might do until we meet again, to keep these problems smaller."

If goals have not yet been identified, the therapist can still motivate clients to use the time between group sessions productively: "As we stop today, I would like each of you to watch your day-to-day activities closely until we meet again and notice when your situations are not bothering you as often. Keep track of these exception behaviors and be ready to describe them to the group next time.

To close the first group session, the therapist might consider the following option: Pass out a folder to each client containing six pages, each entitled SOLUTION NOTES and displaying a scale from 1 to 10 at the top and a list of questions beneath it (see page 61). Then ask clients the following questions:

- If a 10 means that you are in charge of your life and a 1 means the problem is in charge of you, where would you say you are today on the scale?
- Where would you like to be before our group meets again?
- What did you learn about yourself today in group that would help you get there?
- Does anyone have a suggestion for any particular group member?

Clients can use their Solution Notes to keep track of their progress during and between group sessions. They should be encouraged to take their folder home and make notes specifically during the times when their lives seem to be more on track. (Have more Solution Notes forms available upon request for future sessions so that when the group series ends, clients have a wealth of information within their folders.)

THE SECOND GROUP MEETING

The solution focused therapist begins the second group session by asking, *"Who would like to start our time together by telling us what's gone better for you since we last met?"* Thus, the therapist ensures that the group session begins with a familiar tone and follows the same format used in the first meeting. If clients do not have many improvements to report and prefer to talk about what did *not* work, the following statements from the therapist may help them get back on a solution track:

Tell us about your worst day. Now tell us about a day that was slightly better than that.

Let's suppose that more of that happens. What do you want to happen for you by the time we see you again?

In spite of things being rough, you still came back to the group. What do you all think that says about this member?

I'm really not surprised that your progress is taking more time. The events that brought you to our group last time were quite challenging. I wouldn't be surprised at all if your change is slow—yet steady. We will be here for you as that process continues.

SUMMARY: THE SOLUTION FOCUSED GROUP SESSION AT A GLANCE

The five major points for therapists to remember in conducting a solution focused therapy session are listed below. Each is followed by a representative comment therapists can use to ensure that a therapy session remains solution focused.

1. Set the mood for focusing on solutions:
    *   *Give us a brief idea as to why you are here and what you want us to know.*
2. Suggest goal setting.
    *   *What will you be doing in the future that will tell us that things are better for you?*
3. Search for exception behaviors.
    *   *Tell us in detail about the times when things were better for you.*
4. Encourage motivation.
    *   To individual client: *What will you be doing more of as these problems dissolve?*
    *   To group: *What will we see this group member doing more of as problems dissolve?*
5. Task development.
    *   *From our conversations about when things were better, what will you each try doing for a week that might help you begin to approach your goals?*

SOLUTION NOTES

Problem is in control of me   *I am in control of problem*

1   2   3   4   5   6   7   8   9   10

Week of _____

1. *Circle your current status on the scale above.*

2. *Where did you move on the scale from last week? List below how you managed to do so:*

    _____

    _____

    _____

    _____

3. *If you stayed at the same level as last week, list how you were able to stay stable:*

    _____

    _____

    _____

    _____

4. *If you moved down the scale slightly, list below what you did previously to move forward. What have you done in the past that was successful in a similar situation?*

    _____

    _____

    _____

    _____

5.   *What have the significant others in your life noticed about you over the past week? How did that affect their behaviors toward you? (List names!)*

_____

_____

_____

_____

_____

_____

THERAPIST'S SOLUTION NOTES

Exceptions noticed by therapist during group session:

_____

_____

Scaling Question: How far has client progressed and on what actions is this rating based?

    Problem is in control   *Client is in control*

1	2	3	4	5	6	7	8	9	10

What seems to work best with this client in stimulating participation and ensuring a good response in the group setting:

_____

_____

CONCLUSION

Solution focused group therapists have a unique opportunity to encourage their clients to see themselves differently by changing the context of the group process from a focus on *problems* to an attempt to discover *solutions* that lie within each individual. The questions in this chapter for therapists to ask group clients are merely suggestions. The best questions will develop spontaneously in the group process as the therapist follows clients in their conversations, noting the *exceptions* that emerge and translating these into solutions.

After the group therapy session ends, the therapist should document information that was received by observing and listening to the clients during group interactions. *The Group Therapy Case Notes* is an organized way for the group therapist to stay solution focused when thinking about the client afterwards and designing a strategy for working with the client during the next group session. The case notes also assist the client's case manager in a treatment setting to identify the client's goal, exception identification leading to new strategies and the client's task between group sessions. Such information can also be used to assist a treatment team in an agency to decide further treatment for a client, a school counselor in a school setting to refer a school client for outside help or to remind a therapist in private practice of each client's concerns.

GROUP THERAPY CASE NOTES

(Case Management)

Client: _____ Date: _____ Group: _____

Goals of therapy according to the client:

_____

_____

_____

_____

Exceptions (to client's problem) identified by client during group session:

_____

_____

_____

3 Disease Versus Habit:
Group Therapy Ideas for Out-of-Control Behaviors

Treat people as if they were what they should be,
and you help them become what they are capable
of becoming.

—Johann Wolfgang von Goethe

In Chapter 2 I tried to show that our own beliefs and how we think about change affect not only our role as therapists but also our interactions with our clients and ultimately determine the extent of our respect for our clients. For example, therapists who label chemical dependency as a disease will treat a chemical dependency group and its members as diseased and in need of prescriptive interventions to survive. The notion of incurability that often accompanies the labeling of a condition as a disease has significant—and disabling—results. Perhaps most pernicious is that families and significant others begin to doubt that a return to normalcy is a reasonable expectation. Descriptions of symptoms seem to serve as answers for those feeling crippled by their condition, yet descriptions do not offer solutions.

According to Webster's New Twentieth Century Dictionary (2nd Edition, 1983) *disease* is defined as "a particular destructive process in an organism with a specific cause and characteristic symptoms." Therapists working from a disease focus with clients may seek out traditional ways of helping clients control disease. For example, clients are cautioned to avoid various destructive behaviors, such as drinking, using drugs, starving themselves, or engaging in promiscuity. Dealing with clients who apparently find security in such negative behaviors may involve confrontation, inpatient psychiatric treatment, or day treatment, all responses that seek to direct clients to face up to their disease in the hope that this will discourage them from these destructive behaviors in the future. When clients do not comply, they are said to be in denial or not ready for change. Many therapists who work from a disease model see such clients as unwilling to be helped. Therapy is often stopped at this point, and clients are often told that there is nothing else for the therapist to do until they are ready to change.

Solution focused therapists have a different belief about the activities that negatively influence a person's life. They perceive their clients as stuck in a habit that has temporarily disabled their life, leaving them feeling lost in symptoms that seem insurmountable. According to *Webster's New Twentieth Century Dictionary,* (2nd Edition 1983), *habit* is defined as "an act repeated so often that it has become automatic with a person." Whether the client is an adolescent who uses marijuana every weekend or a woman who binges three evenings a week, the solution focused therapist views the client as being steered off track and in need of ideas to get back on track and out of the clutches of the habit. The therapist holds the belief that habits are not born with people but, rather, develop over time in response to some personal need. This idea allows the therapist to see clients as wanting normalcy in their life but being unaware of the strengths they have and the things they can do to regain stability.

A group therapist who regards negative behaviors as habits will search for "exceptions" to those times when a client's habitual behavior occurs and will encourage group members to do the same for each other. Viewing group members as having the resources to find their own direction to stay habit free encourages solution focused therapists to persevere in their attempts to discover within each group member those situations in which the habit does not prevail. The solution focused approach gives group members a chance to see their situation as temporary and encourages them to openly discuss the times when destructive habits do not take over their lives. A kinship develops as group members begin to identify with each other's success in discovering what works in fighting the habit versus what allows the habit to win.

The ideas of solution focused brief therapy can be refreshing to therapists who work with day patients, inpatients, or private clients in individual or group therapy who have problems that are sometimes thought of as out-of-control behaviors. These include such habits as problem drinking, drug abuse, anorexia, bulimia, panic attacks, and anxiety. For the purposes of this chapter, many of these problem descriptions are referred to as out-of-control behaviors/habits because of their acute and dangerous nature, not because they are always beyond the control of the client. Many of the habits described in this chapter are life threatening and affect the client's life in ways that threaten health, relationships, and employment. Whether the therapist thinks of the behaviors as disease or habit, the reality of the habit's impact on the client's life does not change. The days of the medical model of mental functioning are passing. Understanding and gaining insight into problems from the past was at times validating and relieving to clients, but managed care now insists that therapists move more quickly with the treatment process and become more goal oriented. In short, today's therapist must help clients identify behaviors that will relieve them of problem symptoms without necessarily understanding how they became trapped in a problem.

COMPARING APPROACHES TO GROUP THERAPY

In the following sections the differences between a traditional *problem-focused* medical model and a *solution focused* approach to psychotherapy are briefly explored.

THE MEDICAL MODEL APPROACH TO GROUP THERAPY

The following points characterize the medical model approach to group therapy:

> The treatment team or treatment assessor discusses the patient's *deficits* and *diagnosis* and plans strategies to solve the patient's problem by placing the patient in a structured group therapy.

> The patient is *not* seen as capable or competent to attempt or solve the problem independently. It is hoped that group therapy will help the patient confront the problem, deal with identified issues, and gain insight.

The patient is given *consequences* when inappropriate behaviors exist and is told how to change these behaviors. *Restrictions* are imposed until the behaviors are controlled.

Group therapy focuses on problems that the physician, staff, and nurse see as needing to be solved. The staff sees such *resolution* as vital to recovery from the disorder.

The patient is expected to gain *insight* into the source of problems and to respond to confrontations with a change in lifestyle, since it is the patient's lifestyle that is viewed as dangerous.

The patient is expected to see the need for ongoing group therapy, considered the only means of maintaining recovery from the problem.

The goals and activities of group therapy that are developed and instigated to solve the patient's problem are based on what has helped other groups before with similar disorders.

The patient is encouraged to *confront* and help fellow group members face their problems by directly communicating likes and dislikes of what others say or do not say.

Discharge plans occur after progress is seen and when the patient is close to terminating group therapy.

THE SOLUTION FOCUSED APPROACH TO GROUP THERAPY

The following points characterize the solution focused approach to group therapy:

The treatment team or treatment assessor discusses the exception behaviors that are noted during assessment and determines the group therapy *collaboratively* with the client. The goal is to create a group context in which the client will learn more about personal abilities and then learn to solve personal problems independently.

The client is viewed as one who is capable of functioning independently but who has overlooked personal abilities and assets because of the problem's interference. Group therapy is regarded as a means of assisting the client in recognizing competencies that will result in a redirection.

The client is viewed as needing a break from the problem. If the client is taken over by negative behaviors related to the problem, the therapist urges the client to tell the group about previous behaviors that worked at times to avoid or minimize the problem.

The client is *not* expected to gain insight in order to solve the problem. Instead, group clients are encouraged by the group facilitator to reflect on more successful actions in the past and to share those strategies with each other as a means to resolution of problems in the present.

The staff, therapist, and physician (if the client is an inpatient) listen not only to each other's observations but to those of the client as the latter states the personal goal for group therapy. Groups and activities are directly correlated with the client's goal for treatment and are collaboratively chosen so that the client is in charge of the program.

Discharge planning occurs in the admission interview and its goals are the goals of group therapy.

MOVING PAST THE MEDICAL MODEL TOWARD SOLUTIONS

You can't hold a man down without staying down with him.

—Booker T. Washington

A comparison of the two models for group therapy is provocative, for it shows the difference between relying on a person's competencies and giving the staff full responsibility for solving the person's problem. Even the descriptions of people in treatment are different—patient versus client. The solution focused approach is collaborative, intimately involving the client, whereas the medical model involves primarily the opinions and ideas of the mental health experts. While the medical model has assisted many persons with change through insight, under-standing, support, instruction, and practice, it has been my experience that people tend to relapse most readily when they are given staff-designed tasks that they are uncomfortable with or that don't fit with their lifestyle or personal goals. While staff members mean well in designing tasks, the ultimate motivation toward change still lies with clients, who will not cooperate until they are comfortable with new strategies.

GROUPS FOR PEOPLE WITH EATING DISORDERS

Deena was in a group for people dealing with unhealthy eating habits. She recounted the desperation she felt each time she decided she would stop buying ice cream. Her treat to herself for working hard was a dish of ice cream, sometimes as many as five a day. When she "overate" by consuming other sweets as well, she would make herself exercise for hours to compensate for the added caloric intake. After having tradi-tional inpatient treatment for her eating disorder, where she was moni-tored twenty-four hours a day, Deena found that her unstructured life outside of treatment did little to stop the bingeing, which began again shortly after her discharge from the program.

When she began coming for group therapy, Deena's original goal was to "just cut down," but she felt that her out-of-control behavior was overtaking this goal. She would eat one brownie after another and then ice cream, cookies, or any other accessible sweet and would not stop until all the food was gone. When asked if there were times when her habit was *not* taking her over, she admitted that there were and that those times would always precede her bingeing. After Deena devoted two weeks to watching for the times and places where she ate less, we had the following exchange during a group setting:

> LM: *You know, what I am concerned about is that we are mov-ing too fast. After all, you have told us that eating ice cream in*

particular gives you such satisfaction and I, for one, would not feel right about asking you to give up something that important.

DEENA: But I really do want to cut down; I just don't want to give it all up.

LM: Have you noticed which kinds of ice cream make you gain more weight?

DEENA: I've memorized the calories and fat on all of the cartons. Of course, though, I love the richest, fattiest kind.

LM: Apparently, it must bring you great satisfaction. Does anything else come close to what it does for you?

DEENA: No, just other sweets, maybe listening to music, sometimes, or walking with my dog. The trouble is, if I'm in the house, I'm too tempted.

LM: I have an idea. Please tell me if I am off base after I share it with you. You said that you eat ice cream about five times per day, right?

DEENA: Yes.

LM: How much would you suggest cutting down on or changing your eating habits so that you would feel just a slight improvement?

DEENA: Maybe eat it just four times a day.

LM: Okay, and when you do eat it, I want you to truly enjoy each bite, since it is so satisfying to you. Notice the texture, the flavor, the taste, the richness and eat it very, very slowly so you can enjoy each spoonful like never before.

DEENA: (Smiling) I can do that.

The group didn't see the importance of our collaboration at first. Many of them felt that recovery from an eating habit could only happen if the food was given up completely. I responded by noting that sometimes when we greatly enjoy an activity and then are threatened with losing it, we cling to it even more. I speculated that this occurs because the activity is so important to us. I asked the group, "Have you ever found yourself struggling with trying to do other things besides eating when you are upset?"

Here are the responses from members of Deena's group:

"I cling to people."

"I buy more things when I'm upset."

"I overdo activities, almost to the point of obsession."

"I work more at my job."

"I sleep more."

"I just sit and watch television more."

"I keep doing things for others and neglect myself."

I responded to the group as follows:

These activities obviously give you pleasure at times when you need them. To ask you to give them up would be cruel. Instead, for the next week, I would like all of you to think about what Deena is doing and imagine what it would take for you to come back next week and tell us that you had changed your eating habits just slightly while still enjoying the activity of eating. I'll be anxious to hear how you will feel about yourself.

As group members took on a new view of their habits, control over these habits increased. Deena was the first client to leave the group. As she said good-bye, I asked her to tell the group what activity she had found to be the most helpful in the group process. She said that the group had helped her cut down on her consumption of ice cream by helping her realize that when she was busy with other activities she ate less. She said that she saw ice cream as an escape from boredom and that now that she had more things to do, she ate less. She also said that she appreciated the fact that she was never told to quit bingeing.

THE WEIGHT LOSS EXPERTS:
A NEW VISION OF ANOREXIA

While writing this book, I read an article in the *Family Therapy Networker* that illustrated how a solution focused group therapist might think about anorexia: "We muster every strategy and technique to disarm the eating disorder, which we view as life threatening, unlike the client who sees it as lifesaving" (McFarland, 1997, p. 38).

Of all the issues brought to individual therapy or group therapy, the eating disorder is perhaps the most frightening to the therapist. Life is often at stake by the time the client arrives in therapy, sometimes accompanied by well-meaning family members who are fearful of losing their loved one. Control issues are of utmost concern to the client, who may see the therapist as the enemy wanting to take away control. Because of the severity of the eating disorder and of the determination of those with such a disorder, it seems appropriate for the therapist to give control to the client up front so that resistance is lessened and the client feels secure. To such a client, the solution focused therapist would deliver a message such as this one:

> In no way do I intend to take away from you the control you have over your life. I respect your actions as those designed to help you feel better about yourself. Please see me as someone who wants to help you to be healthy again—on your terms. It is my hope that we can work out ideas together that make sense for you. I am only interested in your having a long life.

I have found that the words *eating disorder* are best not mentioned in solution focused group therapy. The connotation of *disorder* is that the person needs to be repaired. That idea tarnishes people with an eating problem and may even exacerbate the problem by giving them reason to believe that they are out of control. Rather, describing the problem as "a habit that discourages health" is more appropriate in a solution focused group for those with compulsive overeating, anorexia, or bulimia. The following case is an example of how changing the description of her problem gave control back to a young woman struggling with anorexia.

Kim, age eighteen, weighed seventy-five pounds when I first met her. She was already beginning to experience chills, amenorrhea, and hair loss. Her physician had become alarmed when her parents brought her in for a physical after she returned from her college freshman year in Paris. Clothed in several heavy shirts during the heat of summer, she relayed to me her fear when she looked in her mirror the night before and saw her ribs. Although she was frightened, she was not yet fearful enough to begin to eat heartily; she said she was very concerned about gaining weight, because she had once weighed over one hundred thirty pounds and did not want to reach that weight ever again. She reported that since all the foods in Paris contained fatty ingredients, her diet there had consisted solely of apples. She described her parents as over-protective and financially stressed and mentioned a brother who had strayed into drugs, disappointing the family tremendously. A bright college student who had made all A's during her first year abroad, Kim described the years prior to college as stressful and competitive, having attending an elite preparatory school where she felt like an outcast. As the conversation continued during our initial group assessment session, I learned the following about Kim and her goals:

- She wanted to raise her low self-esteem, which she felt had developed from her efforts to become the perfect child after her brother had so disappointed their parents.
- She was fearful of food and saw only fat grams in whatever food was presented to her by her well-meaning parents, which resulted in her refusal to eat.
- She wanted to be healthy again but not fat.
- She wanted to get back into life, but she wanted to control how she did so.
- She knew there was a problem with her eating habits, but she did not want to describe it as an eating disorder.
- The act of counting calories and pieces of food was helpful to her because it gave her a sense of control.
- Weight gain would have to be a gradual, controlled event for her; she was willing to gain weight—but slowly.
- She said she wanted me to respect her need to be thin yet healthy.

After several individual therapy sessions, Kim stabilized her weight loss and slowly began to eat fat-free, healthy meals, which she chose to eat on a daily basis. Her parents desired a quick weight gain program, but I spoke with them (with Kim's permission—indeed, insistence—and with her doctor's approval) and cautioned them not to push her to gain weight too rapidly. Kim said she wanted to gain weight at her own pace, and I agreed that this was a good idea, reassuring her that she was indeed "a weight loss expert." I mentioned casually that should she regain her weight too quickly, she would certainly know how to lose it again. She had, after all, lost fifty pounds during one year, and that feat convinced me that she would know how to control any weight gain that got out of hand. Kim shyly agreed that she had this expertise and admitted that she continued to count calories. When she occasionally asked me if this practice was acceptable, I always responded with the question "How does it help you to eat more healthy foods?" Kim always replied, "I feel more in control."

Eventually, it became clear that the times when Kim ate (her exception behaviors) were the following:

- When she knew the exact caloric intake of each item.
- When she planned her meals for the next day, making sure that one meal was not as high in calories as the other two.
- When she ate alone, a condition that made her feel relaxed and therefore more likely to eat.
- When she felt organized in her day.
- When her parents backed off about her eating habits and said nothing about the fat-free foods she ate.
- When she recalled how seeing her ribs had frightened her.

Kim gained thirty pounds during our visits over the course of the next nine months. She became vibrant and healthy, yet I continued to refer to her during our therapy sessions as the expert on weight loss. This continual reminder that she had control made an impact on Kim, for when she eventually entered a support group, she began using the same phrase with others who struggled with the same issue of control.

The following ideas and questions suggest a collaborative way of tackling the problem of the group client who is dealing with anorexia, bulimia, or compulsive overeating. They imply respect for the client's choices while the attempt is made to redirect the client toward health.

1. Listen first and empathize with group members' need to overeat, starve themselves, purge, or use laxatives. Set a pace for goal setting that is realistic and respectful by commenting as follows:

    It sounds like you are often taken over by your eating habits, causing you pain in your life. Imagine with me for a minute that in the near future you will be more in control of your eating habits. Tell me, what will be different in your life and what will you be doing when you are in control?

2. Search for "exceptions" and client strengths that might overcome the habit by asking questions such as these:
    *   Can you take me back to a time when you experienced just a little difficulty from your eating habit?
    *   What were you or the significant others in your life doing at that time that seemed to make a difference for you?
    *   How would you explain your ability to be in control during that time?

3. Assist group members with task and strategy development by posing the following questions:
    *   When you give in to the habit, what does your behavior do for you?
    *   What else in your life has given you a little of the satisfaction [or however the client describes it] you get from your eating behavior? [What else? What else? What else? Keep asking this question so that more exception behaviors emerge for later task development.]

4. Assess clients' status and progress by referring to the 1-to-10 scale:

    On a scale of 1 to 10, with 10 meaning you are controlling your eating behavior and 1 meaning that the habit is controlling your life, where would you say you are currently on this scale? Based on your goal and the strategies you have used before to control the habit slightly, what would you suggest doing for only a week to move your position on the scale more toward a 10?

Group members who are medically ordered to attend the group may not readily recognize the impact of their eating problem on their life. These members might be assisted by asking the following questions:

- What activities or situations are you deprived of due to the presence of the habit in your life?
- What relationships are strained or distanced due to the habit?
- How does the habit keep you from being the person you want to be in your life?
- How do you encourage the habit to take over at times?

WALKING THE WALK OF SOLUTIONS: FREEDOM FROM DRUG AND ALCOHOL PROBLEMS

Believe that life is worth living, and your belief will help create the fact.

—William James

In their groundbreaking book *Working with the Problem Drinker* (1992), Insoo Berg and Scott Miller mention the following view on problem drinking:

In contrast to the traditional model, we do not believe in *alcoholism* per se and, for this reason, do not feel that the pursuit of a single treatment strategy for all cases of problem drinking is either logical or useful. Instead, we have come to believe that there are many alcoholisms—perhaps as many as there are problem drinkers (Berg & Miller, 1992, p. xix).

John, age thirty-three, came to group therapy in response to an ulti-
matum issued by his parents. He had moved back home after losing his
eleventh job in three years. Financially strained, he depended on his
parents for shelter and food. Occasionally, he would become bored and
sell some item of worth to buy alcohol, which he would binge on for
days at a time at a friend's house. He would then return home, where his
mother and father would lecture him and nurse him back to health. John
described his life as nothing but torment. When he entered group therapy, he told group members that he would not go to AA (Alcoholics
Anonymous) and to forget about giving him a lecture. He talked at
length about how he wanted his life to be. I acknowledged his apparent need to drink to numb the pain from difficulties he had experienced
in his life over the past five years: his wife had left him for another
man, he had repeatedly lost jobs, his property had all been repossessed,
and his health was failing miserably. John *knew* that alcohol was the
culprit. I attempted to help the group step into his world and also to let
him know that we were trying to understand. At the end of the first
group session he said, "This is the first time I have met a counselor who
did not scold me. I know I have a problem . . . I never needed anyone to
tell me. Here I feel like you can really help me because I'm not embarrassed to tell you about all of the stuff I have done. It seems like you
understand."

At least it seemed to be a beginning for John. Over the next few
group sessions, he talked of times when he had not been drinking and of
the activities he enjoyed during those times. He was a black belt in
karate, and during his nondrinking times he would work out and feel
good. He also described how he used alcohol to help him sleep. According to his earliest memories, he was too hyperactive to sleep well. It
seemed that alcohol relaxed him into a three-to-four-hour sleep each
night. I referred him to a sleep disturbance clinic for evaluation. During
one session, while he was processing other "exceptions," John looked at
me and said, "I seem to binge when I am hiding my booze. I was so
afraid my wife or my mother would catch me, I would drink and drink to
hide it." This realization led him to conclude that if he were on his own
again, supporting himself, he might not feel the need to hide his alcohol

and might have a better chance of regaining his sobriety. John began searching for a job, found one, and earned enough money after two months to move out of his parents' home. The drinking slowed to one or two drinks a weekend, according to our contract, and John began working out again in a new karate studio.

John stopped coming for group therapy when his life improved. I did not hear from him for over a year—until he called to tell me that he had relapsed. Our phone session consisted of recalling what his former strategies had been and my complimenting him on his initiative to call me and get back on track. He joined a new chemical recovery group of mine shortly after our phone conversation. It was fascinating to hear him describe how he had kept his job over the past year, but John at first focused only on how he had failed. He had difficulty giving himself credit, yet the group was able to compliment him on his commitment to keep his job and on his concern for his parents. Through group observations John eventually learned that he needed to socialize with the coworkers who he had previously thought were out to get him and to begin working out in a new karate studio. Whenever he revealed to the group his fear of being close to a person at work, the group reassured him that they enjoyed his company and suggested that he follow his own instincts. The group seemed to help solidify his immature beliefs about his competency and to assist him in believing in himself.

The kind of realizations that John came to about himself and his ability to cut down on his drug and alcohol use are not uncommon when therapists use a solution focused approach. This approach seems to help clients feel less threatened, less like failures, and more like survivors. Besides—think about it—people use drugs and alcohol for a reason. One of the first questions I ask people in chemical dependency groups is "What does it do for you?" They are surprised by this question, yet the answer is of great value to both client and therapist. Clients immediately feel understood, and I use the information to understand their needs, later helping them identify more appropriate behaviors they can use to satisfy their needs. Besides, people struggling with drugs and alcohol abuse are often searching for ways to stop pain in their lives or to deal with such problems as insecurity or loneliness. The following case is another example of using the solution focused approach with a client whose problem involved alcohol abuse.

Several years ago I served as facilitator for a multifamily group for teenagers who were enrolled in a day treatment program for depression. I recall how a daughter attempted to help her father see the strain his drinking put on the family. Previously, the family had tried to convince him that he was an alcoholic. He denied such allegations, saying that he provided them with a good home, food, and clothing. On this occasion, with other families present, I asked the members of this family, "How do you wish things would be for your family in the near future?" The daughter again attempted to help her father see how desperate she was to have a normal family life:

SARAH: It would be normal . . . like everybody else's.

LM: What would it look like, Sarah, someday when it is normal?

SARAH: I could depend on my father to take me to the place I asked him to the day before, without his forgetting. He would spend time with me instead of drinking at night. He wouldn't yell at my mother.

LM: Have things always been this way?

SARAH: For the past few years they have. Before then, it was better when he had a different job.

LM: So it sounds like a problem has invaded your household in the past few years. How has the problem changed things?

SARAH: Like I said, he forgets, he yells.

LM: What do other people do when the problem is around like that?

SARAH: My mother cries and yells back. I get mad at Dad, scream at him, then I go to my room and get depressed. My little sister acts up.

LM: If everyone in your family were to begin fighting the problem on a small scale, what would you each imagine yourselves doing?

MOM: I guess I wouldn't listen to his yelling. I would leave the room when it starts instead of yelling back. I probably would stop buying the beer.

SARAH: I think I would go out with my friends more and not stay around to be as depressed.

AMY: I think I'll stay away from Daddy when he is drinking instead of asking him to play with me. He doesn't like to do it then.

DAD: I guess I could try drinking less at night. I still don't think I have a problem, but it sounds like everyone else does. I love them all and I really want them to be happy, especially Sarah.

LM: Dad, it sounds like the problem has caused you to do things that you don't like. How would you like things to be for your family?

This change of focus from seeing Dad as the problem to interpreting the *problem* as being the problem helped lessen resistance and increase opportunities for family dialogue to occur that was more loving and effective. In addition, the group situation gave other families an opportunity to experience a lesson in family systems theory, learning how an individual member's behaviors can influence an entire system and then change it.

Gaining the cooperation of group clients who are caught in the web of chemical abuse is vital, especially when such clients may be feeling out of control or when employers or significant others in their lives are demanding sobriety. While working in an adolescent inpatient unit for several years, I became acutely aware of the torment that behavior modification caused in adolescents who would not cooperate with the program. Placed in treatment for six months at a time, those adolescents were supposed to learn a lesson and stay straight for all the "right reasons." Too many times, relapse occurred with patients who "talked the talk" but did not "walk the walk." After I observed group confrontations, family-of-origin weekend retreats, and various outside support groups, it occurred to me that we walk a fine line as therapists in asking people in pain to stop behaviors that bring them some sort of peace and tranquillity in a world that only they can understand. The nerve of us! No wonder some of them do not cooperate. No wonder we feel frustrated.

In the past, therapists dealt with alcoholism or drug abuse by confronting clients until they admitted their powerlessness and accepted the label of "addict" or "alcoholic." While many people achieved positive and healthy results from such a process, there were others who did not respond. It is that population in particular that is often helped more effectively in solution focused group therapy. The following ideas and questions serve as a guide for group therapists who treat clients bothered by drugs and alcohol:

1. Attempt to understand group members' need to use the substance. Step into their world and become their partner against the substance by asking:
   - What has drinking or drugs kept you from succeeding in and enjoying in your life?
2. Assist clients in visualizing life without the problem. Suggest that they think about how others will view and relate to them when the problem dissolves, a technique that will help them develop goals:
   - What will you get to do when drugs or alcohol is no longer a concern for you and others in your life?
   - Who will probably notice first that the concern is gone and that *you* are in control and not the drugs or alcohol?
3. Explore clients' past attempts to gain control over the substance, while acknowledging the difficulty in beating a habit that was useful in some ways yet harmful to health, job, family, and relationships:
   - What have you tried in the past to control the drugs or drinking?
   - When did you last find yourself in control of the problem with drugs or alcohol?

   Ask all group members for all their strategies and list them on the board for everyone to see. Keep asking "What else?" until there is a long list of "exceptions" and strategies. Afterward, go through each strategy and determine whether or not the strategy worked to defeat the drinking or drug problem. Strike out the strategies that were not successful. Leave only the "exceptional strategies," including those that brought even slight relief from the problem; these become the first of many solutions for clients to examine. Then ask each contributor of a strategy:

- How were you able to accomplish this?
- Who was there, where were you, what was different in any way?
- What were you believing about yourself at the time that might have made a difference?

4. Invite group members to dream of a time in the near future when the problem is not as influential in their lives as it is at present. Use presuppositional language to illustrate to members that change will happen:

- When things continue to get better for you and you are in more control of the problem that placed you in our group, what will you be able to do that you've been unable to do?

5. Assist group members in developing tasks and strategies by asking them to rate themselves:

- on a scale of 1 to 10, where 1 means that they are taken over by the effects of drugs or alcohol and 10 means that they are in control of the substance. Then pose the following questions:
- Where were you when you began coming to group?
- Where are you now that we have talked about overcoming the problem?
- Where would you like to be by next week? How will you get there?

For clients in partial programs or day treatment programs, the following additional question is helpful:

- What can you do just for this evening, based on what you have told us that worked slightly in the past, to move yourself up the scale just slightly so that you are more in control of drugs or drinking?

For those in inpatient programs, the following question is helpful, particularly if discharge from the program is imminent:

- What do you imagine yourself doing when you exit our program that will tell you and those important to you that you are more in charge of your life?

CONCLUSION

Thinking differently about out-of-control behaviors does not minimize the severity of a problem nor discount the diagnosis of a disorder. This chapter simply offers a fresh perspective on such behaviors, a perspective that lessens the impact these behaviors have on a person's life, freeing that person to believe that life can change. Thinking of substance abuse as a dangerous habit instead of a disease affliction promotes hope and helps both therapist and client talk about the situation more comfortably by lessening embarrassment. Instead of thinking of themselves as crippled by a problem or diagnosis, group clients in therapy for substance abuse can perceive their lives as reparable and are thus more likely to move forward and live their lives differently.

4 The Survivors' Club:
Overcoming Sexual Abuse

Experience is not what happens to you; it is what you do with what happens to you.

—Aldous Huxley

I believe that people have the ability to heal and move forward in their lives after experiencing abuse. This belief has evolved from witnessing the successes of many clients who were able cope and move forward in spite of their terrible experiences in abusive situations. It wasn't easy for any of them, but many were able to develop good relationships, get married, have children, and become successful in their careers. Some of the survivors told me that it helped to face their perpetrators and scold them for the harm they had caused. Other survivors said that they simply moved silently away from those who hurt them and wished for a better life, even when it meant moving far away from their families. While the memories never totally disappeared, they dimmed in influence over their lives. The determination of these survivors to have a better life never stopped; it guided them forward into lives that they once thought were impossible to have. They are some of the bravest, most amazing, and competent people I will ever know. They are the true teachers of survival.

This chapter introduces new ideas for thinking differently about sexual abuse survivors. These ideas evolved from my experience in working with clients who had been unsuccessful in therapy based on a pathological model to resolve the impact of sexual abuse and who found peace when they began to perceive themselves in a different way. The light that began to appear at the end of the dark tunnel of sad memories often became brighter after the first session. I learned that proposing to people that the abuse can be viewed as just a tiny part of a very long life made a difference. It was very rewarding to watch them step back into life and away from shame.

FOLLOW THE LEADER: GROUP CONVERSATIONS FOR NEW BEGINNINGS

As a therapist in private practice, I have listened to many sad stories of clients who lived for twenty, thirty, even forty years after enduring an abusive situation without revealing their experience to anyone. When these clients came to therapy, it was to talk about *other* problems. Sometimes the abusive situation was brought up as we co-constructed their genogram. Other times clients cautiously mentioned an abusive situation as a fragment of their life story that they wanted desperately to forget. Whatever path the client chose, I followed her, the leader, cautious to never suggest that another problem was the result of abuse or that she face her perpetrator. Many clients convinced me that their chosen paths over the years had brought them success in other areas and were better approaches. So I listened and respected their judgment completely. To redirect them to talk more about the abuse seemed disrespectful. Instead, I chose to assist them in realizing their abilities to cope with life during those times. I invited clients to step behind my eyes and reconstruct new perceptions of themselves.

When clients choose to talk about an abusive situation in their attempt to understand *why* it happened to them, the conversation is often accompanied by shame and doubt, as if they felt responsible in some way for the abuse. (The word *situation* is a term that I often suggest to clients in reference to abuse, one that seems readily accepted by them.) The haunting questions of their lost innocence may always go unanswered, and when I hear questions from clients such as "Why did it have to happen to me?" I usually reply, "I don't know. All I do know is that *you* did nothing to cause the situation to happen to you. Tell me, if you did know why it was done to you, how would that help you step back into life?"

Clients answer this question in a variety of ways. Some report that they would feel less guilty. Some say that they would be reassured if the abuser knew he or she was wrong. Others say that they would finally relax and know that they did nothing to provoke the violent actions. Some reply that it would be a big relief to finally just know and have the abuser face them and admit what he or she did. However clients respond, I continue our dialogue by saying, "Suppose you never do find out *why* this awful situation happened to you. Suppose you never face the person who hurt you. *What else* could happen in the near future that would help you to begin feeling more reassured, relaxed, or relieved so that you could move forward into your life, even slightly?" And then the dialogue turns toward "exception" gathering, and I ask, "When has a little of that happened to you during the past few weeks, months, years? Where were you, what were you doing differently at the time that was better?"

These questions suggest to the client that while the reality of knowing *why* the abuse occurred may never be resolved, moving forward may still be possible without such resolution or confrontation. Maybe there are other paths to take to move into the present without the hauntings of the past. Yvonne Dolan, therapist and author of *Resolving Sexual Abuse* (1991), says of alternative therapies for sexual abuse resolution:

> Having a victim of sexual abuse tell and retell the tale of her victimization for the sole therapeutic purpose of desensitization is like removing a bullet slowly and painfully, one tiny millimeter of metal at a time, reopening the wound each time. This form of desensitization is not always dependable; even in the cases where it does succeed over time, it is often an inefficient and unnecessarily painful method of treatment that prolongs the client's suffering and revictimizes her over and over again. (P. 29)

If the solution focused process is to *assist* clients in moving forward in their lives, it makes sense that whatever means the therapist uses in group therapy would best be guided by the client's own wishes. Often those wishes are *not* to retell the story. This is most respectfully done when therapists are working with clients who have lived with the secret of an abusive situation for most of their lives and who choose to continue to move forward without recollection. Such deliberate coping skills should be verbally recognized by the therapist for the client in the group therapy setting; by setting this example, the therapist opens up opportunities for more support from other group members who honor the client's decision to move forward without having to relive the past.

In his book *Residential Treatment* (1993), Michael Durrant, therapist and author, suggests ideas about behavior and how it can be altered. The description below may have a message for therapists who are working with sexual abuse survivors on how to assist them in making sense of themselves differently, so that life can be lived differently:

> If behavior is influenced by context, the meaning of behavior is not fixed, and people are not as predictable as our systems of classification might suggest. A focus on context is a focus on meaning, and meaning is not a fixed entity. I do not believe that therapy or residential treatment should be about identifying some recognizable problem and modifying people's behavior or dealing with the underlying causes. I believe therapy should be about establishing conditions in which people can make sense of themselves differently, and thus respond differently. (P. 10)

How, then, can therapists create a therapeutic environment where group clients can make sense of their lives in ways that motivate them to live in the present without the influence of abuse constantly haunting them? Certainly, group clients should introduce themselves and explain what brings them to group therapy so that the therapist can learn how they view themselves. The therapist may initially ask the following of the group:

> As we introduce ourselves to each other today, I would like to ask each of you to tell us what you think we ought to know about you. Please do not feel that you have to tell us any details

you do not feel comfortable sharing. In this group it is not necessary to tell us everything to move forward. Instead, we want
to respect your privacy. Just tell us enough so that we can
understand why you came today and what you hope to gain
from coming.

Long and specific descriptions about past abuse should not be
encouraged, according to Dolan, unless the client seems to heal from
such dialogue, and that can be verified by asking the client how such
descriptions are helpful. If a client goes into details that begin to make
some group members uncomfortable, the group therapist can respectfully say, "You are telling us many details that have made you very sad.
How does it help you to tell us some of the details?" Some clients think
that such recollection is expected and that it will help them bond with
other group members. These clients should be respected and listened to,
then respectfully and kindly redirected toward the present. After the
introductions are complete, suggestions from the therapist on developing a new success story will help direct clients toward changing perceptions of themselves.

NEW STORIES, NEW CHARACTERS, NEW BEGINNINGS

David Epston suggests that "writing success stories transforms the relationship of the person or family to the problem, as well as the person or
family's relationship to the therapy. It has the effect of distancing persons from the problem and it enables them to 'consult' to others as well
as themselves should the problem re-emerge in their lives" (White &
Epston, 1990, p. 163). Changing the description of clients who have
experienced abuse from *victim* to *survivor* can serve as a beginning for
the solution focused group therapist to employ within the group situation. The way the therapist thinks about the clients will come across in
the group conversations and create the context for perceptions to change.
The following guidelines, suggested by William O'Hanlon of the Hud-

son Center for Brief Therapy, serve to reinforce the ideas and exercises in this chapter:

- Find out what the client is seeking in treatment and how she will know when treatment has been successful.
- Ascertain to the best of your ability that the sexual abuse is not current. If it is, take whatever steps are necessary to stop it.
- Don't assume that the client needs to go back and work through traumatic memories. Some people will and some won't. Remember that everybody is an exception.
- Use the natural abilities the client has developed as a result of having to cope with abuse (e.g., disassociating, distracting). Turn the former liability into an asset.
- Look for resources and strengths. Focus on underlining how they made it through the abuse and what they have done to cope, survive, and thrive since then. Look for nurturing and healthy relationships and role models they had in the past or have in the present. Look for current skills in other areas.
- Validate and support each part of the person's experience and past.
- Use symbolic tasks and objects to help mark transitions from the past and to help externalize the problem or some experience to be worked on.
- Make provisions for safety (written contract between therapist and client) from suicide, homicide, and other potentially dangerous situations.

MIRROR, MIRROR ON THE WALL: INSTRUCTIONS FOR A GROUP EXERCISE

Group therapy with sexual abuse survivors can enhance the quality of life for group members through support and encouragement. Many times clients come to therapy with a preconceived notion that they are *used goods* and will be forever tarnished by the situation that happened to them. The next exercise is appropriate for use in the first group therapy session with sexual abuse survivors. The exercise will enable the therapist to set the stage for future conversations in the group sessions, focusing on competencies of the clients instead of their victimization.

The therapist can duplicate and present the "Mirror" worksheet to each group member. Before beginning the exercise, the therapist should read out loud the passage at the top of the worksheet by Carlson. Ask group members to comment on what Carlson is suggesting about living one's life in the present. Suggest that there are many roads to take in life and whatever road we choose to take and how we think about ourselves as we travel can influence our experiences. Then, reading the worksheet with the group, ask members to imagine how they would like their lives to be a month from now. Ask them to be very specific with actions, not just emotions. Ask them to write their answer next to *New Ideas (Goals)*. If a group client cannot verbalize how she wants life to be, ask her to imagine specifically how she does *not* want life to be and then write down the opposite or what she would like instead. To assist in setting goals, Dolan (1991) also asks her clients, "What will you think your significant other would say your first small healing sign would be . . . and your next small sign of healing?" (p. 33). With this question, Dolan in effect has the client temporarily borrow the perspective of someone who cares about her.

Explain that part of the exercise involves two columns with the headings *Victim* and *Survivor.* Ask group members to imagine how they would specifically be accomplishing their goals toward the next month if they thought of themselves first as victims and then as survivors. (It may be helpful to ask group members to cover the *Survivor* side with a piece of paper as they respond to the *Victim* side and then cover the *Victim* side while responding to the *Survivor* side.)

After the exercise is complete, discuss with each group member what she would like to begin believing about herself, just until the next group meeting, that she feels would help her function more as a survivor. Ask group members to write down a task that might show those new beliefs and indicate that the tasks will be experimental. An additional assignment might be to ask group members to watch for other experiences before the next group session where the new belief helped them to act differently.

After group members complete this exercise, it may become apparent to them that holding on to victim beliefs and behaviors of the past makes goal setting and planning strategies for the present very difficult. This is the point of the exercise. If it is successful, group members will view themselves and each other as survivors, not victims, and that view will be reinforced by the therapist.

WHO'S THE MOST POWERFUL OF ALL?
A CASE STUDY OF DETERMINATION

Sadly, there will always be clients who come to therapy with a long list of symptoms that seem to prolong their unhappiness in life. Lost in a world where victimization is imposed upon them by legal authorities and then scoffed at by those who want them to "just move forward," the survivor seeks strength and justice but is sometimes inhibited by revenge and discouragement. When such clients come for treatment, an individual session or two is often helpful before group therapy is suggested. Understanding their need to be heard is of the utmost importance in these cases, for it begins to give these clients what they deserve and what was denied, namely, respect.

Caroline, age twenty-two, was date-raped by an athlete after a fraternity party during the last semester of her senior year of college. The experience was her first sexual encounter. She was physically as well as emotionally injured. After she reported the incident to police and was examined at the hospital for bruises and abrasions, it was suggested that she seek counseling. Caroline described the visits with one of her first therapists as very depressing and unhelpful:

> He kept asking me each week to tell him about what happened to me, over and over. I never understood why he did that. I always felt much worse later. He also told me that I felt more shameful because I was too religious. He put me on an antidepressant and some antipsychotic drugs, which did nothing. I cried constantly with the medications and was always so angry. He told me it was time to move on, but I never could. Everyone

MIRROR, MIRROR ON THE WALL:

A Group Exercise

"To a large degree, the measure of our peace of mind is deter-mined by how much we are able to live in the present moment. Irrespective of what happened yesterday or last year, and what may or may not happen tomorrow, the present moment is where you are—always!" (Carlson, 1997, p. 29)

1. *With this quotation in mind, imagine how you would like for your life to be one month from now. You will still have the same people and circumstances in your life, but your actions would not be as influenced by the situation that brought you to our group. Write your new ideas of how life will be below:*

    New Ideas (Goals):

    _____

    _____

    _____

2. *What we believe about ourselves in the present can affect our actions. Below are two columns. As you think about your goal, as stated above, imagine how you would be reacting, acting, or be-lieving about yourself if you thought about yourself as a* victim *while trying to reach the goal. Write down those thoughts below the word* Victim.

    How would you react, act, or begin to believe about yourself as you pursued your goals, as you begin to visualize yourself as a sur-vivor? Write your answers below the word Survivor:

Victim	**Survivor**

Reaction/Actions:

Beliefs:

Feelings:

3. *Which description, victim or survivor, seemed to be most helpful as you thought about accomplishing your goal? In the space below, write down the actions, reactions, or beliefs that will help you move* slowly *into your present goal, just until the next group session:*

Task

_____

_____

_____

_____

4. *In what other situations in your life have you successfully used these actions, reactions, or beliefs? Consider times at home or work and interactions with children, friends, or family. How were you able to do this? What would others say you did? Please be specific.*

_____

_____

_____

_____

_____

did the same thing. I would tell them that I was not going to give up until Joe [the perpetrator] was indicted, but no one seemed to want to help me. Instead they just kept telling me to stop thinking about it and get on with my life. The more they told me that, the madder I became. Pretty soon all I did was go to work and hate men. I would come home and watch television and argue with my sister. We started to hate each other.

Feeling victimized by the legal system and having reason to feel victimized by other professionals, Caroline began to take on the characteristics of a victim. She lived the victim role each day, believing that her life was forever altered and that people looked down upon her. Even worse, she began to think that people did not believe her story. During her last months of college, many of her friends in the fraternities on campus had turned against her after the assault, accusing her of wrongful accusations against the perpetrator. Some of her close friends questioned her determination to file charges, even her family discouraged further legal action and told her that it was time to move forward. In spite of these pressures, Caroline was able to graduate that semester with an A average and tutor other students in English, her major. After graduation she moved two hundred miles away to a small city where she obtained a job at another university. As she spoke to me of her sad experience and then of her efforts to move away from the university she had graduated from, her strengths and ability to function in such a horrific situation became obvious to me.

When I asked Caroline how she had been able to complete her college career and move so far from her family after her traumatic experience, she said that all of her life she had been a very determined person who rarely stopped for anything once she put her mind to it. She said that perseverance was a nice distraction for her when she was troubled, that when she was upset with a situation, she often overcommitted herself to other activities. Caroline's inexhaustible pursuit of justice while she struggled daily with frustrations from the legal system, with the fear of seeing the perpetrator when she visited her hometown close to the campus of her alma mater, with her fear of future abuse, and with depression, sleeplessness, fatigue, and distractibility taught me that I needed to cooperate with her determination if I was to be helpful.

The story Caroline had constructed with the encouragement of others was that of being a victim. The victim role she took to heart kept her isolated and feeling sad, threatened, and fearful. To make things worse, important people in her life doubted the severity of the event and attempted to push her into recovery too soon. This actually encouraged the opposite to occur, for Caroline began to embrace her victimhood for all to see in order to save face and become more believable. When people take on certain characteristics in order to make their story more vivid to others, they sacrifice their chance at being successful in life in order to be more understood by others.

From her description, Caroline seemed to want desperately to stop living within an unhappy and unsuccessful story, yet she was having a very difficult time writing a more successful one. In order to assist her, I needed to consider the following two exception behaviors she was revealing to me in our first session:

- She was strong and competent enough to finish a semester with high grades in spite of a traumatic event.
- She was willing to persevere for justice in spite of the discouragement of others.

In an effort to cooperate with Caroline, it was also important that I respect her current needs and beliefs about the situation:

- She was not ready to move forward in her life. Only she would know when she was at that point.
- She desperately wanted others to know what happened to her, so that her embarrassment would dissolve and the perpetrator's guilt would be told.
- She wanted to be helpful to other women as a result of achieving justice.

Obviously, any attempt to move Caroline forward before she wanted to go would not be well received. She had made that clear. However, I did see her as stuck in the victim role and unable to pursue the justice she desired. I knew that as long as she thought of herself as a victim, she would remain isolated and distant.

During Caroline's last semester in college, after the situation occurred, she had been active and visible on campus. She said she had distracted herself by staying busy and tutoring students while filing charges against her abuser. As I identified these strategies, Caroline acknowledged them but did not see the relevance in using them in her current situation. With this in mind, before the first session ended I presented an idea to her for consideration. I took a large piece of paper and drew a time line. I asked her for her exact age when the "bomb" (her description of the sexual assault) went off in her life. I then asked her how long people tended to live in her family. She said many of her relatives had lived a long life, to an average age of eighty. Looking at Caroline, I took a marker and beneath one end of the time line I wrote the numeral 22 and beneath the other end the numeral 80. Then I drew an × on the line to represent the bomb.

×	
birth 22	80

Then, moving my marker very slowly from the 22 across the time line toward the 80, I made the following comments:

> On the scale that I have drawn here, I want you to envision, as we look at it together, how a year has already pushed you away from the bomb. You will never go back, Caroline, to that bomb because now you know too much. You are too educated and cautious now. The bomb is already over 365 days farther away from you than it was on that day. We can see the bomb only at a distance. As I move my marker across the time line, I want you to realize something: you probably have almost sixty more years to live without that bomb ever going off again in your life. I would like for you to think about your life in this new way. As you do, imagine with me what you will be doing now that you have stepped away from the bomb and it begins to have less of an impact on your life.

To assist Caroline in beginning to move slowly in her life towards solutions, I then asked her, "What would you and I see you doing, specifically, in a very small way just for the next week or two that would tell us both that you were indeed stepping out of this situation?"

At the next session Caroline told me that she was beginning to have some good days but she would catch herself and tell herself that she couldn't let that happen. She was terrified that if a jury saw her feeling better, they would interpret this to mean that she had not really been hurt. This was dangerous thinking. Her beliefs about how she should appear to others were holding her back from living in the present. As Caroline related her small attempts to move on with her life, outings with friends—during which she would catch herself feeling better and then drift back into a depressed state in order to maintain her victim role—thought of how much I wanted for her to appear as strong on the outside as I believed she was on the inside. Apparently, she did not see the advantages in appearing to be strong and felt instead a need to be weak. I then made the following comments:

> My kids and I take tae kwon do. At times we have to spar with each other, and it gets to be quite interesting. They are obviously better at being fearless than I am, and it truly makes a difference in the outcomes of their matches!
>
> Once I watched two fighters fight in a tournament. I knew one fighter to be a rather weak fighter. When the strong fighter won, I thought, "Well, he really didn't have to put up much of a fight because the other fighter was too weak."
>
> Another time, I watched two strong fighters spar. When the winner was declared, I thought, "He really had to be strong and violent to beat the other guy. The loser really had to put up a fight just to stay in the ring."
>
> I wonder which image the jury might see in you that would convince them that your abuser was very violent with you—the strong Caroline or the weak Caroline?

A week after that session, Caroline reported having a better week. Shortly afterward, she entered a women's group and continued for a month, until she obtained a new job in a large nearby city and moved into an apartment on her own. She called once to tell me that she had enlisted the services of a well-known attorney who had taken her case and was preparing for trial. Caroline was filing suit not only against the abuser but also against the fraternity for having alcohol at a college party, the bar for serving alcohol to underage students, and each athlete who harassed her after she filed charges against their peer. Two months later I received a letter from her describing how her pursuit of justice was being accomplished. She had spoken at a fund-raiser for a candidate running against the incumbent district attorney, who had refused to try Caroline's case. She got up before the audience there and told her story. Caroline's new image of herself as a survivor has assisted her in stepping back into life and has helped her begin dealing with a situation she is now choosing to step out of each day toward the justice she deserves.

When I asked Caroline recently what she will do if the justice she seeks is slightly less than she desires, she responded, "Just knowing that I have pursued it like I have, and that others know what happened through this process, has already begun to give me some of the relief I have wanted all along. I know he may never go to jail, but doing all I have has at least helped to take me out of this emotional jail, and every day I feel farther and farther away from it."

The questions and time line described in this chapter's case study are suitable for group use. The following exercise, which involves creating what I call a "time line to freedom," may be performed in the first group session, after introductions have been made. It promotes a different focus for survivors and resets the atmosphere for the group process toward one of freedom from the problem. The exercise is best begun by the therapist's drawing on a large chalkboard or piece of paper a time line similar to the one below:

---

birth   end of life

At one end of the time line is the word *birth,* representing the beginning of a group member's life; at the other end is the phrase *end of life,* representing the average life span for people in that member's family.

The therapist then asks each group member to think of the amount of time that has lapsed since the trauma occurred, in years (or smaller units of time, if appropriate). Each group member answers in turn as the therapist records names and date of the abuse on the time line.

The therapist then places a mark representing a generalized time for all the traumatic events on the time line and says:

> I am placing a mark on the time line to represent all of your events. As I do so, I want each of you to realize that you have already stepped out of the event, even if it has only been for a few days. I want you to realize that the event can never happen to you again. You know too much and you have come too far. You never have to go back. You have already moved forward.
>
> I want you to imagine with me for a moment, that you have stepped out of the event. Imagine, as you do so, that you now have freedom for the first time from the influence of the event. What will you be able to do, now that the freedom is beginning to happen for you in your life, that you have not been doing since the event occurred?

If a group client has a difficult time verbalizing what she would want to do, ask "What is it that you will want to *stop* doing?" Then ask, "As you stop doing that, what do you hope you will *begin* doing instead?"

As each group member speaks of new actions, the therapist can write these down under the time line, with a client's name next to each new action. The list will be long. After the goals are written, the therapist can ask the group to describe how they can begin to reach their goals on a small scale, that is, just until the next group session. The important assumption of solution focused brief therapy to remember at this point is to go *slowly.*

ADDITIONAL PROCESSING QUESTIONS FOR ASSISTING SEXUAL ABUSE SURVIVORS

The following questions focus on the situation of abuse by externalizing it as an object to overcome and conquer, obtaining freedom from it as a result. This approach frees abuse survivors from feeling damaged and gives them an object or illusion to escape from instead. Therapists who utilize this approach will find it even more therapeutic to ask group clients to name their event as if it were an object. Adolescents or children in survivor groups can be invited to draw the event on paper, name it, and toss it into a trash can; then they draw what they imagine as the opposite of the event to hang on the wall. A scale can also be placed on the wall where the pictures are hung so that during each group session the pictures can be moved according to how group members see their own progress and the progress of others. Sample questions for using this approach are as follows:

I know this is a tough question, but what do you think you do that allows the situation to take over sometimes?

What are you believing about yourself when it takes over?

What do others do that helps the situation to take over? What could they do differently that would help? How can you let them know what to do?

Tell me about the times in your day or week, when you do not allow the situation to take control. When was the last time that happened, even slightly? When was the last time it tried to take over but you stopped it?

What are you doing differently when you are in control of the situation? What else?

Who is the first to notice when you are in control of the situation? How does that person act toward you when you are in control? What are you believing about yourself when you are in control?

Someday soon, when you are no longer troubled and imprisoned by this situation, how will your relationship with a significant person in your life be?

On a scale of 1 to 10, with 10 meaning you are in total control of the situation and 1 meaning that the situation is in control, where are you today? Where would you like to be by the time I see you again?

At the end of this exercise, the therapist might ask the group where they would like to see a particular member be by the next group meeting and what they have learned about that member that might help him or her during the next week to stay in control. Then the therapist should ask that person, "How will you get there, based on what we have talked about today?"

THE MINUTES OF YOUR LIFE: AN EXERCISE

I remember as a little girl going fishing with my father and throwing pebbles into the lake. I loved watching the ripples roll over and over and over again, even though the fish swam away (much to the dismay of Dad!). The ripples always stopped. The pebble, which seemed so small in such a large lake, always slowly sank to the bottom of the lake, to be packed away with the other pebbles and future fossils. Years later, after graduating from college with a degree in geology, I held even greater appreciation for the tiny fossilized leaves and creatures that lay frozen in time. They were part of such a huge system, living only for a short amount of time on earth and then becoming forever a part of its history.

As this chapter concludes, I would like to share one last exercise, brought to my attention by my good friend and colleague Stephen Chilton. This exercise is dedicated to Dr. Glen Jennings, a professor who influenced many of my ideas about sexual abuse and Chilton's ideas about the abilities of clients to move forward after experiencing abuse. Dr. Jennings told this story in one of our graduate classes:

If you follow the traditional way of thinking about sexual abuse, that the abuse can influence the entire life of a person, that way of thinking mires the client in a *problem* focus and convinces

them that there is no hope. The client can get so mired in diagnoses and labels that she cannot get out.

Life is really like a big circle. Within this circle are all the
minutes of a person's life. His birth, childhood, adolescent-
hood, adulthood, family life, job, friends, schooling, etc. These
events make for a really large circle! If we think of the "event"
of sexual abuse as a dot on a vast sheet of paper, or as a pea on a
very large plate, or one very tiny circle in a very big circle, the
pea or dot is the one moment in time that a person was abused.
While the moment was tragic, it was one moment amidst a sea
of millions of moments in a person's life. Thinking in this way
offers hope . . . that somewhere in that circle are other memories that deserve more prominence and focus.

This exercise can be presented as a group exercise or as a closing
conversation. Draw a very large circle, explaining that it is the circle of
life that we all experience. Invite group members to imagine that all of
their years of experiences are inside the circle. Ask members to remember the joys of their lives, no matter how small, and to think of the experiences they are thankful for; the people who have given them love,
hope, and friendship; the careers that have helped them to feel successful and important; and all the objects of their lives that they cherish. All
of those experiences are inside the circle. Place a tiny dot off center
inside the circle and describe that tiny dot as just a moment in time in a
very large, fulfilling life. While the moment was tragic, it was a moment
that can be pictured as a very tiny moment in a very large lifetime.

Ask group members to think about and discuss the following
questions:

When you think of the situation that brought you here as just a
tiny dot in a very large circle, what other events does that give
you more time to appreciate about your life?

With this in mind, let's imagine that tomorrow morning you
awoke to think of the large circle as the whole of your life and
the small dot that we have drawn here today. As you moved

through the day, what would you be doing differently, just for tomorrow?

When you look at all the space around the dot and think of it as all the minutes when you were able to believe better thoughts about yourself, what kind of thoughts come to mind that you would rather think about?

CONCLUSION

Several years ago I had the opportunity to work in a group for sexual abuse survivors with a young woman, age twenty-four, who was married to a man who sexually abused her on a regular basis. The young woman told the group that she and her husband had been childhood sweethearts and that the abuse occurred only after they married. Currently separated and fearful of more abuse, she struggled with how she was going to have to say no to reconciling with him one more time. She was a successful elementary school teacher who also worked part-time at a dry cleaners to distract herself from the situation and avoid her husband. This strategy was exhausting her. I commended her for her strength and showed her the time line, inviting her to think about how life could be when she stepped out of the abuse, fear, and exhaustion she was feeling. As our session ended, I asked her what we did that might have made a difference. She replied, "I never realized that it was even *possible* to permanently get away from this until now."

Two weeks later the young woman returned to the group to tell us that she had been confronted by her husband to reconcile, had turned him down, and had filed for divorce. She told us that she had quit the part-time job and was beginning to enjoy the pool in her apartment complex for the first time without fear. She apparently had become assertive enough to place a restraining order on her husband, who finally was leaving her alone. She then told the group that she had answered an advertisement for a national airline, had applied for a flight attendant position, and had been hired on the spot. She said that the group session would probably be her last because she was due to begin training in two weeks. Her statement as the session ended was this: "I realized now that I have never *really* lived. I moved from home to marriage with someone who hurt me and scared me every day. I know now that I don't have to live that way, and I'm off to see everything I've missed. Thank you."

People heal from sexual abuse when given a context to relate to and perceive themselves differently in. John Lennon once said, "Life is what's happening while we're busy making other plans." Assisting sexual abuse survivors to live in the present instead of dwelling on traumatic experiences in the past gives them a new image of themselves and fosters beliefs that make it easier for them to plan for tomorrow.

5 Releasing the Strength Within: Resolving Complaints of Depression, Anxiety, and Phobias

To endure what is unendurable is true endurance.

—Japanese proverb

Thomas, age fifty-six, called our office and said that he needed to be seen immediately because he had attempted suicide the week before. When he arrived for an Employee Assistance Program assessment, he told me about a lifetime of challenging and very sad situations. He described being abused as a child and abandoned by his father. He had married twice and had a son from his first marriage with multiple physical and mental disabilities. His wife abandoned them both after learning of her son's disabilities. Thomas stayed with his son at the hospital every day for a year, working only at night to support himself and his new son. Thomas reared his son until the child was able to be placed in a home for the seriously disabled; then he arranged employment that allowed him to be near his son. Thomas was determined that he would never repeat whatever "mistakes" he might have made in choosing a relationship that had landed him in this lonely situation.

Eventually, Thomas became director of the facility where he was working. He married again and had three more children. During that time he also became ordained as a minister. Living two lives, as minister and administrator, Thomas admitted to overworking and giving too much of himself, but he said it brought him much joy. During those years, his first son died at age fifteen.

In spite of all the years of very hard work, Thomas's business failed. When one of his children became addicted to drugs and another child died, depression began taking over his life. He felt it building up until one evening, a week before he made his first therapy appointment, he attempted suicide. As he sat in my office, Thomas impressed me with his kind, calm, but very tired demeanor. Many thoughts and questions occurred to me as he spoke of a lifetime of incredible challenges:

What kind of strength did he possess that enabled him to nurse his disabled son and keep a job, scarcely caring for himself?

What does it say about a man's character that he chose to tailor his entire life and his business around his son's needs and not his own?

How did he manage to stay alive during the past week, feeling as troubled as he does?

How did he accomplish so much—being a father, a husband, an administrator, a business owner, and a minister—in such a short life?

What is he teaching me as he talks about who he is and what makes him persevere in his life?

Thomas said he would be willing to try antidepressants to help him get back into life; he agreed to talk to his family physician that afternoon and get a prescription. He had just formed another company to support himself and his wife, and the new business was floundering because he was so tired and depressed. Our conversation continued as follows:

LM: How will you know when the depression that brought you here is getting out of the way so you can continue with your life?

THOMAS: I'll be back at work, getting my crews out so we can make some money for a change.

LM: What else?

THOMAS: I'll be back in church. I haven't preached in three months. I miss being there with my people. I guess I won't be thinking about killing myself, either.

LM: I'm so glad to hear that. You sound so important to so many people. How would you explain the fact that you were able to stay alive during the past week?

THOMAS: I'm a God-fearing man, and when I realized what I had tried to do, I thought, "God wouldn't want this for me; I can't do this."

LM: That sounds very supportive for your staying alive and being with those who need you.

THOMAS: My mother needs me, too. She lives with my wife and me because she has Alzheimer's and she keeps me on my toes. I'm so tired. She wears me out following her around all day.

LM: How will you know when things are better for you, Thomas?

THOMAS: Like I said, I'll be able to give again.

People like Thomas would have been labeled co-dependent in some circles. Thomas could have been seen as being *too* responsible, allowing others to depend upon him and deprive him of his health and well-being. That explanation would have accounted for his feelings of being overwhelmed and exhausted. However, the dialogue suggests that his joys in life came from *giving* and feeling useful. Suggesting that he needed rest instead of more work would have been like taking away his soul, yet I wanted this gentleman to have the opportunity to rest and re-gain his health. While I struggled internally, his message of what made his life worth living was getting clearer in my thoughts. I was concerned about his health, but he was more concerned about others. I reasoned that telling him to rest would possibly make him feel guilty and that the guilt would then probably not let him rest. But telling him to rest for the sake of helping others might, I felt, have a better chance of working.

LM: What will it do for you, to be able to give again?

THOMAS: It makes everything click for me. I get joy from help-ing a parishioner, a friend, my wife. She's tired too, from taking care of my mother and me.

LM: It sounds like you miss doing things for others.

THOMAS: That seems to be the worst part. I feel like unless I'm doing something for someone, I'm just not a whole person. You're right. But I've been so tired, I just couldn't.

LM: So, if you came up with some ways that you could feel physically better, so that you could get back into life—so that you could help others—what would that suggest to you?

THOMAS: A long nap! I did that yesterday, as a matter of fact. Pure exhaustion. I laid down and did not wake up until this morning. I feel better today.

LM: Okay, so it sounds like you are already discovering some-thing: that rest will earn you some minutes that you can use to help others. If I gave you a scale, numbered from 1 to 10, and 10 meant you were back into life, giving and helping, and 1 meant that you were so exhausted that you simply couldn't help anyone, where would you say you are now?

THOMAS: About a 4.

LM: Where would you like to be by the time I see you again?

THOMAS: A 6.

LM: What would you tell someone else in this situation to do so they could make it there?

THOMAS: Rest and take care of yourself.

LM: Good idea. What would that look like, by the way, for you?

THOMAS: Well, when my wife goes to bed, I probably ought to go to bed with her. It's just that I always feel so guilty from not doing enough, I can't sleep. My mind just races.

LM: Good idea. I'd like to add one more thing to that: I'd like you to help someone important to you each day before I see you again. It can be anything, big or small. Probably small wouldn't be such a bad idea until you feel better.

THOMAS: Really? That's okay? Because there is this older man in my parish who is really down and out. I was thinking about going over to see him after I leave here.

When Thomas returned the next week, he mentioned that he had tried the antidepressant medication once, felt ill, and then decided to stop after discussion with his physician. He described having a better week, with more energy. He said he had preached at church on Sunday and that he realized that unless he took care of himself, he couldn't preach anymore or help others. He had enrolled his mother in an adult day care program and had asked his wife to go to dinner for the first time in months. He joined a process group for adults struggling with depression and had made a large difference in the group with his supportive and positive approach; he continually told the members to take care of themselves as well as they would take care of others.

USING SOLUTION FOCUSED GROUP THERAPY TO RESOLVE DEPRESSION

Thomas's case is important because it illustrates how cooperating with a person's depression can lead to a simple solution. When people become troubled by problems like depression, anxiety, or phobias, their first desire is to *cure the problem,* so that their current lifestyle is not disrupted. Frustrated and worried, clients seem to view their situation as being problem caused and problem oriented instead of a signal that life is off track and needs readjusting. Many clients think that their feelings and actions will have to change drastically in order to be able to function as well as they did previously. This common way of thinking leads clients to psychiatrists for prescriptions for medication and then to therapists for strategies that will get them back into their normal routine again. Thinking in this problem-focused manner often leads to frustration and fear of failure when the medication does not work fast enough and the therapeutic strategy does not resolve the problem immediately.

Just as an insomniac might try without success to force himself to sleep, so might a client, thinking that this is the *only* avenue to happiness, attempt and fail to force himself out of a depression. Perhaps it would be more helpful for therapists to explore with clients how depression, anxiety, phobias, and grief might be symptoms that are relaying the message that life is not working with their current plan. Thinking in this way lessens the pressure that many clients impose upon themselves when seeking relief from these situations. Some of us may recall the kind parent, teacher, or best friend who comforted us in childhood when we were upset just by saying, "I understand. You have a right to be sad. It's happened to me too." The power of this empathy can release the strength within clients to view themselves as actually being able to withstand the current stress, even though they are uncomfortable at the moment. The therapist can then utilize clients' strengths to help them see that depression is a *signal* that something's missing. In the following excerpt, James Redfield, author of *The Celestine Prophecy: A Pocket Guide to the Nine Insights,* talks of the importance of recognizing symptoms as fortuitous messages that need our attention:

> Why, for instance, do we wake up one morning thinking of an old friend only to get a call from this very person later in the day? Why does a casual meeting with a certain person at a certain time often lead to great advance in our careers, our relationships, our awareness of inner talent?
>
> The Swiss psychologist Carl Jung called this phenomenon *synchronicity,* the perception of meaningful life coincidences. . . . We are not here in this life merely by accident, playing out a meaningless drama. Our lives have purpose, a sense of destiny. (Pp. 3–4)

Thomas Moore refers to depression as a gift, though most clients may have a hard time viewing their sad feelings as being much of a gift. In his book *Care of the Soul,* Moore writes of a priest, Bill, who after sixty-five years of faithful, dedicated service is asked to leave the diocese. At first depressed, Bill later felt rage when he thought of all he had sacrificed for others during his priesthood. Moore describes his work with the priest as follows:

> My therapeutic strategy, if you can call it that, was simply to bring an attitude of acceptance and interest to Bill's depression. I didn't have any clever techniques. I didn't urge him to attend workshops on depression or try guided fantasies to contact the depressed person within. . . . I simply tried to appreciate the way his soul was expressing itself at the moment. . . . Eventually Bill's depression lifted, and he took a position in a new city where he worked as both counselor and priest. . . . He was able to help people look honestly at their lives and their emotions, whereas at a former time he would have tried to talk them out of their dark feelings with purely positive encouragement. . . . Care of the soul doesn't mean wallowing in the symptom, but it does mean trying to learn from depression what qualities the soul needs. (P. 150)

In a process group dealing with depression, this manner of thinking offers an exciting opportunity for group clients hearing each other's stories to brainstorm about those things that might be missing from each other's lives. The following exercise sets the mood for a group dealing with depression.

GROUP EXERCISES FOR DEALING WITH DEPRESSION

In the first exercise the therapist reads aloud the following statement to the group:

> What if caring for ourselves in life did not mean that we must always understand why we are depressed but instead meant that we need to research what in our lives might be missing? Where would you begin to find the missing pieces? What if I suggested that the missing pieces could be found on the days where the depression happened less?

As we begin our group today, I would like for you to think differently about the depression that has been bothering you. I would like for you to see it as a signal of warning, that your lives are not on the right track. Our job in this group is to help you find out what it would take to get you back on the right track by discovering what's missing.

The following questions can serve as topics for weekly group sessions. The therapist can write down group members' answers on a chalkboard to illustrate the positive experiences that are currently absent.

As you think about depression as a signal that your life is not on the right track and you pay attention to that signal, what would you identify as missing in your life, causing you to fall off track in the first place?

As you think about this, what could you do on a small scale to begin changing your life immediately, to sort of regroup and regain some temporary quality of life for the moment? Stay as realistic as possible.

What will it look like when you someday soon reach your goal? What will we all see you doing differently?

The therapist may ask group members what they think they will see a particular member doing differently once that person's goal has been reached. If a group member chooses to talk about what would *not* be happening, ask:

Okay, so that would not be happening anymore. What would be going on instead?

How would the significant others in your life have described you or your activities before the depression led you off track?

For clients who talk about how their feelings will change, such as being happier, calmer, more patient, kinder, the therapist can ask:

When you begin feeling the way you are describing, what will we all see you doing differently that will indicate to us that you are back on track?

As you listen to each other, who would like to comment on what else you think your group peers might be missing in life, based on the times they have described as being better?

Take us back to a time when a little more of what you are describing as positive in your life was happening. How long ago was it that you experienced more of that? What were you doing then? How were you able to do that?

As we have been talking, who noticed a change of attitude in some members as they described what worked in their lives before?

What's been missing in your life to keep you from doing what worked before? What feelings, beliefs, or behaviors are missing? What are some small changes that you would have to make so that your efforts to get back on track would be more successful than they are now?

If you were to rearrange your life for the next week so that some of these old, or new, solutions had more of a chance to get back into your life, what would you do on a small scale?

This exercise is an attempt to change the thinking process of group members so that they become more cooperative with the symptom of depression instead of fighting it so desperately. This is one war that is difficult to survive by fighting the symptom only.

In the next exercise, symptomatology from the *Diagnostic and Statistical Manual IV* Criteria for Major Depressive Episode, p. 327, was used to develop a checklist that is client-friendly. Photocopy the checklist and pass out the sheets to group members. Ask them to rate each complaint on a scale of 1 to 10, where 1 means "totally taken over by the complaint" and 10 means "the complaint is nonexistent."

Questions for the solution focused therapist to ask after group members have completed the checklist are as follows:

DEPRESSION INTENSITY CHECKLIST—
A SELF REPORT

Next to each complaint below, rate its intensity in your life. Use the scale below as a guide:

1	2	3	4	5	6	7	8	9	10
Complaint is in total control.						*You are in total control.*			

1. _____ I experience a depressed mood most of the day, nearly every day.
2. _____ I have a diminished interest or decreased pleasure in all, or almost all, activities during most of the day, nearly every day.
3. _____ I have experienced significant weight loss or weight gain when not dieting (e.g., more than 5% of body weight in a month), and a decrease or increase in my appetite nearly every day.
4. _____ I experience insomnia or hypersomnia nearly every day.
5. _____ I feel agitated or slowed down nearly every day.
6. _____ I feel fatigued or without energy nearly every day.
7. _____ I have feelings of worthlessness nearly every day.
8. _____ I have a diminished ability to think or concentrate, or have difficulty making decisions, nearly every day.
9. _____ I have had recurrent thoughts of death (not just fear of dying), or have attempted suicide.

How many of you were able to rate more than three of the symptoms with a 5 or above?

What does that say about your ability to not be totally taken over by depression?

Who would like to share with us how you have been able to do this?

How many of you were able to rate one or more symptoms with a 7 or above? How have you been able to do this?

As you look over the ratings on your checklist, what do you realize about yourself or your lifestyle that you did not realize before you came today?

How will knowing this make a difference in your feelings or beliefs about yourself during the next week?

The objective of this exercise is to illustrate that clients have successfully fought off some of the symptoms and have continued functioning in spite of their depression. Instilling hope of any kind into a depressed client's life can be lifesaving. Solution focused group therapy aims to create an environment in which group clients dealing with depression begin to view themselves not as depressed but as *stuck* in a life that is devoid of happiness at the moment because life's experiences have led them off track.

ANXIETY DISORDERS

To think is easy. To act is difficult. To act as one thinks is the most difficult of all.

—Johann Wolfgang von Goethe

At age thirty-two, Joan had created an executive travel agency that earned over two million dollars a year. Her second marriage was to an equally ambitious and loving man (who had two adult children from his previous marriage), and together they were rearing their two young children, ages three and five. The couple enjoyed traveling extensively with their children and were popular in all the "right" social circles.

When her family physician referred Joan to group therapy, it was because of nonorganic recurring pain in her chest, a tendency to worry uncontrollably, and anxiety about the safety of her children. Joan would often race home from work to perform "home duties" with a vengeance, even though she had a nanny who not only cared for the children but also did the housework during the daytime. Joan's anxiety caused her to be irritable with her husband, who would come home from work and play with the children while she stayed on the phone helping other family members with their problems. Describing herself as "anxiety stricken" and as someone who did "everything for everyone," Joan said what she wanted most from being in group therapy was a new view of her life so that she could slow down and enjoy it. Here's how Joan saw herself and her current situation:

- She felt that she had been taken advantage of by people outside the workplace—mostly family members—and viewed this as the cause of her feeling overextended at home.
- She felt that she had urges to control everything and that it was during times of feeling out of control that the chest pains seemed to appear.
- She wanted to feel less anxious about needing to help everyone, and she wanted to relax at home with her family and be less irritable with her husband.

Joan's first session in group therapy went as follows:

LM: Joan, what would be the first sign that the anxiety you are concerned about is happening less often in your life?

JOAN: I wouldn't have this pain in my chest and this urge to constantly do it all.

LM: What would you be doing instead?

JOAN: Watching my kids ride their bikes . . . sitting down when I come home . . . enjoying time away from work. I would proba-

bly not be on the phone as much at home. My family calls me constantly wanting advice or to just talk, and I feel badly not talking to them, even though I talk all day at the office to customers. My husband is really sick of it. Just when the kids go to bed and we finally can sit down together, the phone rings. It drives me crazy. Then I don't get everything done, and I get into a frenzy. [As she gave us this information, Joan's speech increased in speed and she became tearful.]

LM: Tell me about the times when the chest pains are less likely to happen.

JOAN: They rarely happen at work.

LM: What is it, I wonder, about work that helps them to happen less?

JOAN: I know exactly what's supposed to go on every day. I feel really in control at work. [As she said this, her speech slowed dramatically.]

LM: What does it do for you to know what will go on each day?

JOAN: I'm not sure. I suppose there are fewer surprises and demands.

LM: Are there times at work when employees request more than usual from you?

JOAN: Sure.

LM: What do you do then that keeps you calm?

JOAN: I just go through the motions and give them what they need. I have an excellent staff. They are very self-sufficient, and I trust what they do. They know I am there anytime, yet they really don't push me to do more than I need to.

LM: [To the group] *What kinds of skills and abilities are you hearing from Joan?*

GROUP MEMBER 1: That she does *control everything.*

GROUP MEMBER 2: She does *help lots of people.*

GROUP MEMBER 3: She's doing what she says she wants to do already.

LM: How did you manage to create such an atmosphere of competence among your staff at work?

JOAN: I'm not quite sure. I guess they just know I'm the boss, so they do their jobs.

LM: Have you ever had to say no to a staff member?

JOAN: Sure.

LM: How were you able to do so and keep their respect?

JOAN: [Beginning to smile] *I called them into my office and told them how much I appreciated them but I had to tell them no. I think I know where you're going with this.*

LM: Oh, where?

JOAN: That I should tell my in-laws and my mother no sometimes. I would like to do that.

GROUP MEMBER 2: You need to do that. You take better care of everyone else. It's time for you to do the same for yourself.

LM: Who else in the group has struggled with trying to care for yourself as well as you do for others?

GROUP MEMBER 3: I got physically sick from doing everyone's job two years ago. I realized, though, that after my divorce if I wanted my three-year-old to see me alive, I would have *to slow down and pay attention to my health. It can get that bad sometimes.*

LM: I wonder, Joan, how saying no or taking care of yourself better would make a difference with the anxiety.

JOAN: Well, I could relax at night and worry a little less about how to fix everything.

LM: Sounds like a good idea for the next week. In addition to that, I would like you to do something else. I would like for you to plan in advance and schedule in time with your kids and husband in the evening. You know, plan the evening. Plan for every-thing that might go on, and have a back-up plan if something goes haywire. You enjoy planning and being in control. We might as well cooperate with that.

GROUP MEMBER 1: But that got her in trouble before.

JOAN: Are you saying that it's okay to like to know what's going to go on next? I feel so much better just knowing that I'm not crazy for thinking that.

LM: You are a very successful businesswoman. You have two great kids and have been married for a good while. Your strategies in life may be hectic, but apparently they are effective. Why stop them? Just modify them so that you can get back on track.

Anxiety is a signal that a person is unsure about how to handle a situation. It might be redescribed as a feeling that occurs "when a person is being *too* cautious and is apprehensive about how something will turn out." Whether a person is conditioned from a prior negative experience or afraid of something new, talking about anxiety as a signal meant to tell us something important lessens the person's fearfulness of the situation being faced and thus lessens the anxiety itself.

A woman in a group described having anxiety attacks in the middle of the night. She would wake up, get out of bed, and immediately start pacing. She would be so fearful that she was going to die that she would go into the living room and call her sister long distance, just to have someone to talk to. Upon doing so, she was able to calm herself down, finally relaxing in an easy chair. She would then stay in the chair until morning, sound asleep. Through group conversations the group members pointed out that maybe she needed to get to that easy chair when the attacks began in the middle of the night. The woman decided to try that. Before going to bed, she placed a favorite novel next to the easy chair to read once she woke up and made it into the living room. In one week she began sleeping through the night. She eventually told the group that she noticed being anxious only when she was at home at night. Realizing that her days were free from anxiety, she began to feel confident enough to calmly plan her day without fear and to plan for her nights in the easy chair, if it was needed.

The solution focused therapist can lead clients in a group exercise Anxiety Disorder that involves the use of an "anxiety control" developed from items from the DSM-IV entry for Criteria for Panic Disorder Checklist, p. 395. Before handing out the checklist, have group members rate themselves in relation to the control that their anxiety has over them. For example, say, *"If a 1 means that anxiety rules your life completely and a 10 means that you are in control of your anxiety all of the time, where would you say you are at this moment?"*

After listening to each member's answer, give the following instructions:

> I am going to pass out a checklist to each of you. The checklist will serve as your guide to seeing just how much you are in control of the anxiety that *only sometimes* bothers you. I would like you to rate the symptoms on the checklist in the same way that you have just rated yourselves. For each symptom, place a 1 if you feel that the symptom happens when you are anxious and a 10 if it never happens when you are anxious.

After group members have completed the checklist, the therapist can ask the following questions:

> How many of you were able to rate more than three of the symptoms with a 5 or higher?
>
> Who would like to share with us how you did that?
>
> How many of you were able to rate one or more of the symptoms with a 7 or higher?

ANXIETY CONTROL CHECKLIST

Next to each complaint below, rate its intensity when you have anxiety in your life. Use the scale below as a guide:

1	2	3	4	5	6	7	8	9	10

Symptom always happens.   *Symptom never happens.*

Motor tension:
At times I feel:

1. ____ Trembling, twitching, or feeling shaky
2. ____ Muscle tension, aches, or soreness
3. ____ Restlessness
4. ____ Easy fatigability

Autonomic hyperactivity:
There are times when I experience:

5. ____ Shortness of breath or sensation of smothering
6. ____ Palpitations or accelerated heart rate (tachycardia)
7. ____ Sweating or cold, clammy hands
8. ____ Dry mouth
9. ____ Dizziness or light-headedness
10. ____ Nausea, diarrhea, or other abdominal distress
11. ____ Flushes (hot flashes) or chills
12. ____ Frequent urination
13. ____ Trouble swallowing or "lump in throat"

Vigilance and scanning:
In certain situations I experience:

14. ____ Feeling keyed up or on edge
15. ____ Exaggerated startle response
16. ____ Difficulty concentrating or "mind going blank"

17. ____ Trouble falling or staying asleep
18. ____ Irritability
19. ____ There are times when I am anxious and worry about two or
     more life circumstances, such as possible misfortune to my child,
     who is in no danger and about finances.

What would this indicate about the hold that anxiety has on your lives?

Did anyone feel anxious doing this list?

Did you complete the list in spite of any anxiety?

As you look over the ratings before the checklist and the way you rated these symptoms on the checklist, what do you realize about yourselves?

Knowing this new information, how can you plan the coming week so that you continue to move up on the scale?

Anxious people are often very sensitive, emotional people who want to do things correctly, but their fear of appearing incompetent and out of control inhibit them from doing so in a comfortable manner. As their anxiety increases, these persons lose their rational way of thinking about themselves and actually become physically unable to perform as they desire. For example, when I was in graduate school, I was often required to give oral reports, a task that frightened me very much. I was once involved in a group project where I was to be the second presenter. After our presentations, my professor pulled me aside and said, "Linda, *always* go second. This is the first time I saw you talk to our class in a relaxed state." His comment dispelled a lifetime belief I held, namely, that I was *always* going to be nervous whenever I spoke in public. His suggestion made sense to me. Now, when I present to very large groups, I always make sure I am introduced by someone first. Or I use an over-head projector to show an image on the screen to talk about initially— any technique will do as long as, in my mind, I am the second presenter. For some reason, when the focus is not on me at the beginning, I have a chance to relax and the anxiety disappears.

Therapists should acknowledge their clients' concerns, to show that they believe their anxiety is warranted and understandable but not to imply that clients have to do things differently in order for their anxiety to disappear. The following case from a women's group illustrates this way of being helpful:

Jill, age thirty-three, had been diagnosed ten years previously with bipolar disorder and was taking seven medications. She was convinced that her eleven-year-old son, Matt, was also bipolar because of discipline problems at home. One day in our women's group, Jill mentioned that she had grounded Matt and his sister, Nicole, seven, in their rooms for six hours because they refused to put their Monopoly game away. The group became quite irate at Jill for what she had done to her children and confronted her sternly.

Jill told the group that she knew her parenting skills were poor but that she was bringing both of her children to therapy every two weeks to make up for all of their bad experiences. (Her ex-husband had kidnapped the children three years earlier and had then neglected them for a year before she was able to get them back.) Jill began to cry, saying that she had never learned how to be a good mother because her own mother was always depressed and in bed. She was convinced that she had few parenting skills. I couldn't help but make the following comments:

> Jill, I understand your worry about being a good mother. I need to let you know that grounding your children in their rooms for over six hours is something that you might need to reconsider because it sounds inappropriate. I also know that you want things better in your life with your kids, or you wouldn't be here.
>
> What I am really curious about is how you are still able to bring your son to therapy this week. You don't seem to give up. In fact, you have never missed an appointment, and you are always interested in my questions. You impress me in this way as a good mom who wants to help her children. It just sounds like sometimes your goodness gets covered up when you get frustrated.

The group discussion continued:

> *JILL: Me, a good mom? You can't be serious.*
>
> *GROUP MEMBER 1: Hey, you're doing the best you can. The grounding thing is a bit much but you're getting your kid some help and that says a lot for you.*

LM: How did you manage to get out of bed and bring your son this week and yourself today?

JILL: I just made myself. It's what I have to do to get him well and get me well.

GROUP MEMBER 2: I've been there. It's a very hard thing to do when you can barely stand up. I think she's trying or she wouldn't be here. We need to give her a chance.

The rest of the group time was spent talking about other members' experiences when they were feeling bad but still managed to do at least the minimum for their children. By the time the group session was over, Jill was talking more confidently about what she felt her children needed from her. She called me later that day to tell me that she had found some free summer activities for them to attend. Not only had Jill's spirits lifted, but her children benefited from her renewed feelings about herself.

This case hints at child neglect. In cases such as this, I have found it helpful to be straightforward, as I was with Jill, in order to protect the client and the children. After I gave Jill information about the inappropriateness of keeping her children in their room for six hours, I was able to continue with solution focused questions to steer her in a direction that would help her see better ways to be a good mother.

In situations where I feel worried and tempted to give advice, I think, "What is my goal as a therapist at this moment?" Usually my goal is to help my clients solve their own problems without creating any resistance in them. Confronting Jill about her parenting skills could have resulted in "Yes, but *you* weren't there!" More importantly, it was vital that Jill begin to see herself differently in order to be a more effective parent. I sensed that she needed strokes herself. Defensiveness and resistance eliminate the possibility that new ideas will be well received by a client.

Solution focused group therapists must put aside their judgment and search for the messages being sent by their clients. Jill wanted to be a good parent but felt that her children were driving her crazy with behaviors they had acquired as a result of their experiences with their abusive father. She also said that she could not be a good parent because *she* did not have a good parent. These messages are a far cry from "I couldn't care less about my kids." Thinking about Jill in this way helped to lower my frustration and made me want to search desperately for something she might be competent at. The group followed suit, and soon Jill was taking more positive actions with her children.

FEARFULNESS AND PHOBIAS

Ellen, age seventy-two, was terrified of writing checks in public because her hands shook so badly. Ron, her husband of fifty years wanted desperately to go shopping or on cruises with his wife, but her fear of writing a check or even speaking in a public place restricted her outings to doctors' offices. Ron, a kind and patient man, told me how active they had once been. They had traveled extensively with their four children when the children were young, and they had been traveling together for the past ten years, after Ron took an early retirement, until about six months ago. When Ellen began to develop her fears of being in a public place, Ron attributed it to fatigue and "nervousness." He then began to do everything for her, which, she relayed to me, made her feel even more helpless. She had been an energetic mother and grandmother. To be burdened by "silly" fears made her feel ashamed, and she chose to isolate herself from the world instead of going out and enjoying herself.

In group sessions Ellen explored those times in her life when she had made the transition to a new situation. From listening to her and watching her shyness in the group, I learned that Ellen had always been somewhat shy and that her way of dealing with the shyness was to act reserved and then wait for others to speak to her first. She told the group that at home her hands never shook. She did volunteer work at a church three mornings a week, and her hands never shook there, either. When we spoke in my office, her hands did not shake, nor did they shake in the group sessions. I conveyed to Ellen my curiosity about how she could go into a public place, such as her church or a group therapy room, and stay so calm. When she replied that she did not understand how she was able to stay so calm, I told her that it really didn't matter if we understood it, that it was important that it happened and was encouraging to think about.

Before Ellen joined my women's group, she believed that she would be anxious in any public situation. She had resisted thinking that all she needed was to simply feel confident in order to relax, that all she needed was a little time to look around so that she would not feel watched or threatened. During one of our group sessions, we discussed the idea of noting when and where members stayed calm. The purpose of this exercise was to help clients notice that they were not *problem-saturated* constantly but were, instead, in control more often than they realized, as the following dialogue illustrates.

LM: You have been telling me about a few places that you have visited during the past few weeks where you have stayed calm. Tell me, have you revisited places where your hands shook before, only to find that they did not shake as much?

ELLEN: Last Monday I went to a card shop and almost made it out without shaking. I took my cards up to the desk and began to write the check when my hands started to shake. I had to pay, so I said, "I'll be back in a minute," and went to a chair that was nearby to sit down and finish writing the check. As soon as I sat down by myself, I was fine. The next day I went to buy some slacks. I was kind of worried about things since I had shaken the day before. When I got ready to pay, I wrote the check out before I ever got up to the register and then wrote the rest out on a ledge below the counter. I had looked before I went to the counter to see how I could do it.

LM: You are quite clever! It sounds like it really helps you to scope out the situation until you feel comfortable. I wonder, could this be what happens at church?

ELLEN: Maybe. I remember when I first worked there, I would shake occasionally. I never thought about why I stopped.

LM: I think you really discovered something here, and I am very impressed with you. You could have left but you stayed! What did you learn from your accomplishment?

ELLEN: Maybe that I always need to check things out before I have to get up my nerve to write or shake hands with someone.

LM: I think you should take as long as possible. Don't hurry one bit. Think of it as creating your comfort zone, and don't do a thing until it feels right. There's something else, Ellen, I noticed about you. Other people would just carry cash. Not you. You don't seem to give up. Is this a familiar trait of yours?

ELLEN: My husband and my kids have always said I was quiet but determined. I guess in the past six months, I've thought that I was just giving up by not going anywhere. Now maybe I'm realizing that I just need to give myself more time and not rush into things.

Ellen's contributions to the group process were always welcomed. She added an element of mature wisdom and a real example of the message that a person can accomplish anything she puts her mind to.

Therapy for clients who are bothered by phobias or fears can largely center around identifying "exceptions," especially those that become evident during group sessions. Pushing or forcing clients to take big steps too soon can prove very unsuccessful, since new fears may develop. In my experience, it is more efficient to carefully acknowledge clients' fears, respecting whatever reasons they give for why they are upset. Sometimes a client has no explanation for a fear or for its absence. For example, Ellen's hands never shook during a group session (a group member pointed out this "exception," to Ellen's surprise). When I asked Ellen what her secret was for staying calm, she said she didn't know. Nonetheless, constantly reminding her that she was calm during group sessions and helping her discover other times when her problem was not occurring gave her new confidence.

CHALLENGING BELIEFS: A GROUP EXERCISE

Nothing is so firmly believed as what is least known.

—Michel Eyquem de Montaigne

The following exercise can be used in group settings with clients dealing with social phobias or extreme shyness. This exercise can also be helpful for people who are trying to gain confidence for speaking in public, for being more assertive in relationships, or for asking others for help instead of doing everything themselves. I changed the title of the worksheet from Phobia Intensity Checklist to a less threatening one in order to, obviously, lessen fears! The items on the checklist were developed from the Diagnostic Criteria for Phobias, DSM-IV, p. 417. The therapist using this checklist with group members can begin the exercise with the following comments:

> Some of you have mentioned that there are fears which bother you sometimes. Sometimes fears bother us when we don't pay attention to their purpose. For example, being afraid of something may make you cautious and careful, and those are good traits.
>
> We are going to fill out a worksheet for a few minutes, to see which of the symptoms are *not* happening all of the time. You may find yourselves surprised! This information will be useful for us to know, so that we can build on those times when the fear *doesn't* take over.

After group clients complete the Fear Information Checklist, the therapist should read the first eight items on the checklist individually and inquire about group clients' abilities to score a 1 or above on these items. If any client scores below a 1, treat the sub-score as you would a 1 in the conversation. Here are some sample questions to ask:

> How were you able to score above a 1?
>
> What could explain your ability *not* to allow fear to take over completely?
>
> What were you believing about yourself that got you through?
>
> What's different on days when you would rate yourself slightly higher?

These questions all focus on the client's ability to score higher than a 1 on an item, that is, to avoid being taken completely over by fear. The

FEAR INFORMATION CHECKLIST

Rate the impact of fearfulness on each behavior listed below by using the following scale:

Behavior *always* *happens*		*Behavior* *sometimes* *happens*		*Behavior* *never* *happens*	

1	2	3	4	5	6	7	8	9	10

1. _____ I am unable to continue talking while speaking in public.
2. _____ I choke on food when eating in front of others.
3. _____ I am unable to urinate in a public lavatory.
4. _____ My hand trembles when I write in the presence of others.
5. _____ I say foolish things or am unable to answer questions in social situations.
6. _____ Sweating or difficulty breathing occurs when I am exposed to my specific fear.
7. _____ My fear interferes with my usual social activities or relationships with others.
8. _____ My fear interferes with my performance on the job.
9. _____ I avoid situations I fear.
10. _____ I think my fear is excessive or unreasonable.

therapist should mention that success sometimes wears disguises when it slowly emerges and that group members must watch closely for those successful times.

The therapist should continue gathering information from group members, perhaps writing their answers as *ideas* on a chalkboard so that they can conceptualize strategies together. For example, here are some strategies for speaking in public that were proposed by members of one group dealing with problems of extreme shyness:

Wait for others to speak first.

Talk to only one person at a time.

Always take a friend when you know you will be nervous.

Just go ahead and admit to yourself that you will be nervous.

The therapist can solicit responses from group members by reading a checklist item and then asking speaking questions about it. For example, after reading Item 9 aloud, the therapist might ask, *"If you scored between 5 and 10 for Item 9, how would you explain your ability to face your fear at times?"* or *"What strategies do you use that make facing your fear tolerable?"* Or the therapist might ask, after reading Item 10 aloud, *"If you put between 1 and 5 for Item 10, how would you explain your ability to see your fear as being unreasonable?"*

The questions below use the technique of externalizing a problem, so that the problem becomes the focus, not the person who has the problem. Whether it is a fear of being violent, angry, alone, inhibited, locked in a closed area, or whatever, thinking about a problem as an entity to fight and triumph over can be productive and freeing.

How did you allow the problem to place you here today? What actions do you do at times that help keep the problem alive in your life?

What would your life be like without the "problem?" Who would be doing what differently? What would you be doing differently tomorrow if its influence were less?

What is it like when the problem affects you less? What are you doing during those times? What are you believing about yourself during those times?

If you could visualize the problem, what would it look like?

How do you avoid, at various times, letting the problem take over in your life?

If we wrote a story about your life and titled it "Chapter Two" and you could leave out the problem, what would be different from the current "Chapter One"? Which characters would you omit and which characters would you add to be part of this "Chapter Two"? What are some ideas from "Chapter Two" that you could use gradually now to avoid the problem even slightly for the next week? *[For children's groups, keep the time shorter, such as one to two days.]*

The therapist can also ask the group if they noticed any members who seemed less bothered by their problem during the current therapy session. If the group responds affirmatively, the therapist can ask members to describe the impact on themselves as they interacted with such members.

CONCLUSION

This chapter takes a new focus on mental health concerns commonly found in therapists' offices around the world. The ideas require the therapist to actively redirect the client into a more productive way of thinking. Each client gives us an opportunity to recognize unique traits with which we must cooperate in order for anxiety to lessen and strength to emerge. Regarding anxiety, fearfulness, and depression as *signals* that a client's emotional well-being is under challenge by life can help the therapist cooperate with the symptoms, thus creating a calm environment that begins the resolution process immediately.

6 Solution Focused Family-of-Origin Therapy in the Group Setting

Developed with Terry Hargrave, Ph.D.

Nothing changes more consistently than the past. . . . The past that influences our lives is not what actually happened but what we believe happened.

—Gerald W. Johnson, *Heroes and Hero-Worship*

Imagine a family-of-origin therapist sitting side by side with a solution focused brief therapist and working together with a group. Imagine group members being asked questions about their troubled relationship with their mother and then being asked questions regarding the strengths and exceptions within that relationship. Would the models used by these two therapists—so opposite in their assumptions of how people change, so different in their beliefs of how people accomplish goals and dreams—collide with conflicting expectations, or could they integrate into a framework for change that creates an atmosphere that is friendly yet emotionally charged? Could one model offer the insight that some clients yearn for while the other quickly and respectfully moves the client toward resolution?

These are the exciting questions that Dr. Terry Hargrave, author, colleague, and friend, and I worked on intensely together for a year as we applied them to therapy with individuals, families, and couples. Hargrave was interested in becoming more solution focused, more action oriented. Murray Bowen, considered the father of family-of-origin therapy by many, believed that therapy should "identify the patterns originating in the past that have such a hold on people in the present, and . . . help people unlock themselves." Bowen emphasized "searching out clues from living members of the extended family, especially from older generations, to trace a pattern, and then alter it. To do this, he [used] the genogram, a visual diagram of the family tree going back in time and extending collaterally, with an individual or a couple as the focal point" (Hoffman, 1981, p. 244).

Hargrave saw the value of looking backward but found that some clients became stuck in old meanings and took less action toward change. His desire to become more solution focused led him to the idea of helping clients transform old meanings into new ones, a technique that has the potential to motivate people to act differently. I, on the other hand, was interested in helping those clients who wished to look back at the past do so productively, by finding and developing new meanings from the past that might reveal useful "exceptions" for the future. This approach was eagerly accepted by clients who were curious about past influences but who were not willing to go into detail about negative experiences. My goals and those of Dr. Hargrave, which at first seemed worlds apart, merged eventually into a model that seemed to be emotionally helpful to clients and appeared to be very flexible. Mutual discovery and blending of the language from both models evolved into a new model that gave clients more choices in the therapy process. This chapter, written conjointly with Dr. Hargrave, describes how we were challenged and frustrated by our experiences and discoveries, how we each wrestled with our beliefs, and, finally, how our thoughts merged into ideas and strategies that influenced our clients in a positive way.

ASSUMPTIONS OF SOLUTION FOCUSED FAMILY-OF-ORIGIN THERAPY IN THE GROUP SETTING

Dr. Hargrave and I conceptualized the following assumptions in an effort to develop a framework for our thinking as we worked together. They have been adapted to fit the group therapy setting.

1. It is assumed that a traditional solution focused brief therapy approach can assist people in taking action to deal with complaints or problems. Therapists encourage clients to take action by asking questions such as the following:
   - What will you be doing when things are slightly better for you?

2. It is assumed that traditional family-of-origin therapy can assist people in understanding the meaning of what their families taught them to believe about themselves and about how they were to act in relationships. Therapists can assist clients in this endeavor by asking questions such as the following:
   - When you are believing what your family taught you about yourself, how do you behave?
   - How would you like to think about yourself that would help you do things differently?
   - When you think about the pain that is bothering you today, what do you think went on in your family that helped this pain to grow? How did you think about yourself when this was occurring?

3. It is assumed that meaning is constructed by people and that two basic, consistent constructs are used. The first construct has to do with the individual's belief about the self, which is primarily constructed from how a person is loved. In answer to the question "Who am I?" people believe they are either

lovable	or	unlovable
valuable	or	worthless
precious	or	shameful
special	or	ordinary

   The second construct involves people's beliefs about relationships and the traits required of them in their relationships. These beliefs are primarily constructed through a person's early interactions with caregivers and siblings. When people ask "How should I be in relationships?" they wonder if they should be

controlling	or	flexible
optimistic	or	pessimistic
giving	or	withholding
nurturing	or	self-protective

4. It is assumed that a balance between taking appropriate actions to deal with life and constructing helpful meanings concerning the self and one's relationships is essential for a client's emotional health. If a client does too much of either, the balance is thrown off and satisfaction in life may diminish. In the past, family-of-origin therapy attempted to clarify meanings and assumed that insightful understanding would give clients a reason to change their life. Solution focused brief therapy, in contrast, concentrated on helping clients take actions and assumed that change in any behavior would cause change in another person or situation. When these two basic models are combined, the resulting perspective can be expressed in questions that a solution focused family-of-origin therapist can pose to clients. Below are examples of such questions:

    • How could you begin to think about yourself so that you will act differently in the near future with your spouse? What will you be doing in that situation, specifically?

    • When you think of how you want things to be with your son and how different this is from your relationship with your father, what beliefs would you have to take on so that this new relationship happens? As you construct this new relationship with your son, what would your father see you doing differently if he were watching?

    • How do you suppose you will feel as you teach your child to carry on a new legacy in conducting the relationship between parent and child?

    The balance between efforts to construct meanings and attempts to take appropriate actions, that is, between the family-of-origin approach and the solution focused approach can be expressed by the pairs of constructs below:

MEANINGS	ACTIONS
one's constructed beliefs about oneself	one's efforts to adapt
one's understanding of oneself	one's attempt to be functional
one's perception of relationships	one's behavior in relationships

5. It is assumed that the meanings concerning the self and one's relationships affect the actions one takes in solving problems. The actions taken in solving problems and relating to others serve in turn to construct additional meanings. When people are thinking differently about themselves, new behaviors result and will evolve into new meanings.

6. It is assumed that it is reasonable to think that members of therapy groups can treat each other in a loving, respectful manner that promotes the development of healthy individuals. These group behaviors in turn influence what the individuals believe about themselves and how they interact in group relationships. The group therapist may help group members see that although members of older generations may not want to change their behaviors, group members can change their own behaviors by taking on new beliefs and that these new behaviors will in turn affect their relationships with others.

7. It is assumed that individuals have strengths and resources that give them the ability to develop new and functional actions in order to control dysfunctional and problematic behavior. Understanding and recognizing their strengths and resources is often made difficult for clients who believe that the construction of their personhood was done poorly by their family of origin. When therapists move slowly and help clients recognize that efforts to change their family of origin are actions that are not working, they keep their clients solution focused instead of problem focused. For example, a question asked of a client, who is stuck on confronting a parent regarding past incidents of abuse might be the following:

    • Talking and confronting your mother regarding the sexual abuse caused by your stepdad seems to leave you unhappy and distanced from your mother, whom you say you love very much.

Is this strategy working for you at this time or has it worked in the past?

- What actions on your part would show your mom the depth of your concern to get back into life?

Group therapists can ask the group to describe behaviors that would indicate that specific members were being more productive and stepping back into life.

8. It is assumed that negative programming of one's meanings by one's family of origin can often prohibit one from discovering resources and can, instead, lead to the continued development of meanings that are not helpful or healthy. The group setting offers the client the "magic in numbers," as well as compliments and acknowledgment of the client's competency from others, who have listened to and learned from the client's story. The group, when immersed in a conversation that focuses on promoting new meanings for its members, helps to impose a sort of new family meaning that can encourage a change in beliefs and, ultimately, behaviors.

IT'S THE SAME OLD SONG— WITH A DIFFERENT MEANING

Allowing the solution focused and the family-of-origin models of psychotherapy to blend reminded Dr. Hargrave and me that human beings have basic beliefs about themselves that demand that they place meaning around who they are as persons and how they need to behave. We call the former a person's *belief about self,* and the latter is often referred to as the *motivation* for their actions. The meanings that people place around feelings and actions may be constructed through experiences, but constructing such meaning is innate in humans. Constructing meaning is stable, consistent, and required in order for people to feel good about themselves. The idea that people need to construct meaning in their lives is similar to Chomsky's nativist theory of language acquisition. Chomsky (1957) believes that humans are born with an innate "language acquisition device" (LAD), which makes it possible for the infant to access words of objects and actions and construct them into semantics, syntax, and pragmatics. As infants hear a language, their

LAD makes it possible for them to utilize the language by a set of rules common to all humans. Just as humans come equipped to take in information and utilize it as language, so too do they have an innate ability to take in experiences and form their personhood from them. How children are loved, trusted, treated, and conversed with is taken in and integrated into how they perceive themselves as their life proceeds.

Working within this paradigm, a solution focused family-of-origin therapist can accomplish two things at once:

> Assist clients in changing their beliefs, through redescription and goal setting, by adjusting the meaning ascribed to them by their family of origin

> Accelerate the healing process and help clients take action by creating a context in which they can see themselves living life in the future without the influence of past meanings

These are difficult tasks, because too often individuals are determined to understand before they budge toward a resolution. This is where the family-of-origin therapist sometimes becomes stuck. Group clients have strengths, resources, and abilities that help them adapt to functional new behaviors and control dysfunctional and problematic ones. However, often negative programming from the past prohibits clients from discovering and using their resources and, instead, continues the development of old meanings that are not helpful or healthy.

When individuals have difficulty putting their strength and resources to work in solution focused therapy, it may be that their beliefs about self and relationships are keeping them blind to their abilities. This seems to be what has happened when therapists say, "Solution focused brief therapy did not work in this situation. This person needs long-term therapy!" At this point many therapists do switch gears from solution focused *questions* and adopt another therapy model instead of viewing the client's reluctance as the result of an old *belief.*

Dr. Bruce Khuel's suggestion of a solution oriented genogram (1995) was helpful to Dr. Hargrave and me as we blended our two models of choice. It helped us to help the client whose description of himself kept him shy and uninvolved in life when he realized that in his family of origin, there were indeed others who were more social than he and more satisfied with their lives. It helped the client whose abusive husband convinced her that she was worthless, just as her father had told her years earlier, by discovering within her the strengths of her great aunt. It helped the thirty-year-old man who thought he should have and love a career like his father's when he noticed how his happiest relatives had changed their careers. This was the therapeutic crossroads that encouraged the integration of our model. We asked ourselves

> When their resources are so obvious, what drives unhappy people to clutch even tighter to old beliefs in spite of the danger to their mental health, relationships, profession, and pride?

> When what clients *really* want to do is talk in greater depth about the pain in their life, is it disrespectful to say that they need to look only at the times when their life was better?

Dr. Hargrave and I integrated into individual and group therapy sessions techniques that assisted clients in exploring their past and then hastened their discovery of "exceptions." They left their therapy sessions with practical and helpful historical information about habitual and "exceptional" behaviors; such information could then be used in the present for goal setting, with the help of an additional backward glance toward the past and evaluation of past beliefs. We began to notice that clients were challenging the very perceptions they had clung to for so long, thus opening up possibilities of dealing with family members from a new and different perspective. Particularly in groups, when they saw themselves as strong people who had coped with difficult family members, clients began to see the family members as troubled, not defensive, or as concerned, not overprotective.

Dr. Hargrave talked with group clients about how their lives were circumscribed by meanings imposed on them by their family's trusting or not trusting them, loving or not loving them. The group client seemed to appreciate these explanations, particularly when they were offered by the therapist to another group member. As I spoke with group members about their abilities to cope with meanings in their lives, we discussed the importance of taking into account who they are today and who their family members are, often reaching a consensus to do something different since current beliefs were intruding and preventing them from having the life they desired. When group members heard these ideas, they often seemed almost to sigh with relief in unison. When group clients do not have to be defensive due to past labels or beliefs, they interact differently with each other and exhibit more positive abilities. The following case shows this change of attitude and behavior.

Mary, age forty-five, was a nurse at a state hospital, where she cared for moderately retarded adults, and came to group therapy on a referral from her employee assistance program. In her assessment she was told that she was severely depressed and probably needed long-term therapy since she had been sexually abused by her stepfather from age eleven to age seventeen. In the first group session, Mary told us that she had resented her older brother (who was also physically abused by the stepfather) for abandoning her by leaving home at age sixteen, when Mary was only thirteen. She had kept in minimal contact with her brother over the years, although during the past few years he had contacted her so that she could spend time with her two nephews. Mary told the group that she was gay and that she had just ended a twelve-year relationship.

Mary said that the depression that brought her to the group had accelerated recently, when she tried talking to her mother, age seventy-six, about the sexual abuse. Her mother would not reply to Mary's statements of what had happened, and Mary, instead of feeling better after bringing up the subject, always felt worse after these conversations, similar to how she had felt as a child. She kept talking to the group about her childhood and how her mother ignored her as a young girl. That behavior led to the following group conversation:

> *LM: It sounds as if life was quite difficult for you as a young girl. How would you describe the way your mother treated you?*
>
> *MARY: She ignored me. She turned the other way when I tried to tell her what my stepfather was doing. I remember nights when she would be gone and I begged her not to go but she went anyway. I could never have friends over because he tried to grab them.*

LM: How would you describe the way you were able to stay there and somehow graduate from school and then go on to college?

MARY: I just tried to dodge him whenever I could. I moved out at seventeen and worked two jobs to support myself.

LM: Sounds like you did what you needed to do. How can I be helpful to you today?

MARY: I just want my mother to finally acknowledge that he hurt me and that she hurt me by not doing anything.

LM: What would that do for you?

MARY: Finally give me the peace I need. Somehow I think it will make me feel whole, like I matter. I've never felt like I mattered to my family.

The group wanted Mary to confront her mother, and Mary continued to describe how her efforts to do that seemed to be in vain. The more she pursued her mother's acknowledgment, the worse Mary felt. She had been told by other therapists over the years that unless she confronted her mother about the abuse, she could never go on. I told the group that my impression was that Mary's current strategy wasn't working and that her old beliefs were keeping her stuck. I then asked group members to think about beliefs of their own that they had allowed to continue and that kept them from doing things in their lives that they desired. Here are some of the replies:

"I believed I was ugly, so I would get involved with people who treated me bad."

"I have always thought I was ignorant, so I didn't even try to go to college."

"I thought I should stay at home like my mother did and I hate it but I don't know how to get out of it now."

"I never wanted to make people mad at me; it made me feel too guilty."

"I used to think everything was my fault, so I always apologized first and got taken advantage of."

This dialogue led the group to see how their thoughts and beliefs about themselves not only influenced others but also kept them in old behaviors that they hated. The trouble was, just *understanding* this concept did not give them ideas as to how to change. I knew that identifying "exceptions" to those beliefs would give them opportunities to do things differently, but first they had to be respected for their actions, even those actions that had a negative impact. My dialogue with Mary continued as follows:

LM: What have your strategies been to try and accomplish this?

MARY: I call her and try to talk about it. She won't respond or acknowledge that it happened.

LM: How do you feel when this happens?

MARY: Worse, always worse. Lately all I do is stay at home, by myself. I don't want to be around anybody.

LM: Really, how does it help to be private?

MARY: I like it. I was in this relationship for a long time, and now I just like to be by myself. My friends don't like it when I prefer to be alone though. They keep calling me, but I don't go with them as much as they would like me to.

LM: I was wondering, whenever you talk to your mother and she does not want to talk about the abuse, how are you thinking about her?

MARY: That she still *isn't there for me. She's betrayed me.*

LM: And it makes perfect sense that you might think of her in that way. When you do think of her like that, how are you feeling about yourself?

MARY: Awful, like I don't deserve anything. Lonely, like I don't have a family or anyone to depend on.

LM: What would you say you missed out on while you were growing up, thinking about yourself like that?

MARY: Having friends over, having a family outing, feeling support, and knowing someone was interested in me.

This answer told me that Mary would probably try to hold out for as long as she could to recover those lost experiences. I needed to respect her needs because *she* felt so strongly that they had to be met. Her old beliefs were so painful for her that she couldn't see the resources she did have in her life. I switched over to an exploration of her current lifestyle for a short time in an effort to explore her strengths in other situations. This strategy is very helpful in enlightening clients of their abilities by taking the focus off their problem. It is even more exciting in a group setting, where group members offer several different impressions of the client who is talking. A challenging and interesting exercise can happen at this point if the therapist requests that group members "take a few notes" as he or she talks to the client about more positive times. This means that group members are to listen for statements the client makes that show different, more positive, beliefs about the self. Here is how I handled this exploratory phase with Mary:

LM: You know, you say you work with moderately retarded persons. How do you think about them as people?

MARY: [Brightening] Oh, they are more capable than people give them credit for being. I have often gotten too close to them. [Laughing] I take them bowling or out to eat. People don't realize that they are so capable.

LM: It's so nice to see you smile! Do you think it helps them when you look at them that way?

MARY: Yes, because they know I expect them to do things. They warm up to me and are quite affectionate, more to me than to others.

LM: You seem to have a gift of looking inward at people and seeing more within them. I have an idea; let me know what you think about it. I wonder what would happen for you—just for you, because you deserve the peace you've told me about—if you thought about your mother differently for the next week. Instead of seeing her as a mother who betrayed you, how else could you think of her?

MARY: Well, you know, I know she loves me. She calls me three times a day, sometimes. She wrote this letter here [Hands me a sheet of paper] *and she talks about everything else* but *what happened. I think she is a woman who can't talk about things, because it makes her feel so uncomfortable.*

LM: Are other things uncomfortable for your mother to talk about?

MARY: Oh, yes.

LM: I think you have an important idea. I wonder how it might help you during the next week whenever you talked with your mom and you thought of her in this way.

MARY: I can already tell you I would feel better because I wouldn't bring it up anymore.

LM: Really?

At this point Mary and I talked more about what she had missed during her childhood and what she still felt that she was missing: having a family she could call her own, feeling love and intimacy, and feeling trusted, support and surrounded by friends. She described, again, the abuse and how it robbed her of important years. I drew a time line (described in Chapter 4), for Mary. After we finished talking about moving forward, never to return to the past, she began to smile and relax. The group was very supportive to her as we continued to talk. They were beginning to see the difference in Mary's behavior and language when we switched from talking about what she wanted to change but couldn't to what made her happy currently.

LM: Mary, let's say that it's six months in the future and your mother begins to see you enjoying life in a way that you wish you could have enjoyed as a young child. Let's say she sees you experiencing these three needs you just told me about. What would she see?

MARY: Well, you know, I have two nephews who I really love. I've sort of stayed away from them because my mother is always telling me I need to visit them but they live too close to her, so I don't. I think I would visit them more so I would be a better aunt to them.

LM: What else?

MARY: I need to invite more friends over. I've met someone recently, too. She called me this morning, and it made me smile. I've missed having a relationship like that.

LM: You know, I think you've really got some good ideas to reclaim the needs you had during your childhood. If I gave you a scale of 1 to 10, with 1 meaning you were without any peace at all and 10 meant that you were totally peaceful, where would you say you were when you came in today?

MARY: About a 1.

LM: Where are you now?

MARY: A 5.

LM: [To the group] *Where would you all put Mary as she began talking about the things she enjoyed doing versus the things that she couldn't change?*

GROUP MEMBERS: About a 6.

LM: [To Mary] *What have we done in here that helped you move up?*

MARY: Realizing that maybe it's time to move on and write a new story, like you said, and use the people who are in my life now as part of it.

Mary was instrumental in helping two other women in the group move forward instead of dwelling on what they wished they had accomplished. Using a solution focused family-of-origin approach with clients who were neglected or emotionally abused is instrumental in dramatically changing their thinking about themselves. After group members gather additional information by listening to interactions, they are able to lend more support to further a fellow member's new beliefs.

NEW PERCEPTIONS UNDER CONSTRUCTION

Our clients' construction of meaning for the present determines their perceptions of how others relate to and behave around them, and this in turn determines how our clients behave and relate as well. Mary perceived her mother's actions as those of continual betrayal. She then responded with confrontation and defensiveness. When Mary changed her perception of herself, she acted differently; eventually, her mother saw her differently and became friendlier and more caring toward her.

In situations like Mary's, the solution focused brief therapist has an opportunity to redescribe events and motivate a client to use new strategies, and the family-of-origin therapist has a chance to help a future generation by assisting the current one, that is, the client, in living a better life. In many cases, helping our clients also makes life better for the older generation; instead of turning their back on their parents, many clients are able to construct a new, more meaningful, relationship with them. This seems more motivating, respectful, invigorating, and safer than writing a new story from scratch. There is comfort in familiar surroundings. Changing the decor slightly does not change the floor plan of one's life; it just makes it easier to maneuver through the relationships.

NEW BELIEFS

It is easier to believe than to doubt.

—E. D. Martin, *The Meaning of a Liberal Education*

The solution focused family-of-origin therapist thinks that, for some clients, if there is not a change in personhood, meaning, or beliefs, then changing the client's behavior becomes too difficult and is less likely to occur. Take the case of a client who was sexually abused by her brother.

The person may *believe* that she is "damaged goods" and that she is therefore unable to have a healthy sexual relationship with a partner. In this case, problems persist because the client's basic belief about her personhood keeps her stuck in an old story. In short, her old *beliefs* dominate her current *actions,* making the discovery of her strengths and resources difficult. This leaves the client feeling hopeless and the therapist thinking that the client is resistant or, even worse, *traumatized.* If, on the other hand, this client can modify her beliefs—if, for example, she can see her wariness as an asset that can keep her cautious and careful in new relationships and if she can view herself as a survivor who lived through a difficult event, to which she never has to return—her new perspective might lessen her resistance. In addition, using the time line (described in Chapter 3) can help her free herself from old stories and create new ones around new goals. In a group therapy situation, new stories emerge quickly, as group clients hear the deficits in the life of the abused person and come to her assistance with observations of what has been missing. The group can also help the client understand how being cautious is a positive attribute, not just a reaction to a negative experience.

BELIEF THREADS OF LOVE AND TRUST

One way of thinking about our personhood, or the meaning we ascribe to ourselves through the way we interpret how we were loved and trusted, is to think of two empty spools. One spool stands for relationships and the other for our personhood. As we experience family life, the "belief thread" of love and trust is wound onto both spools. As we develop, we increasingly use this belief thread in the way we think about ourselves and in how we interact in relationships. When a person is having difficulty in putting resources and strength to use in solutions, it may be because these original threads or beliefs are wound too tightly on the spools. Therapeutic interventions in these cases must be designed to successfully wind new threads (new beliefs) on the spool in such a way that they completely cover up the old thread (old beliefs), or else the old thread must be removed from the spool so that new beliefs can be wound around it. Sometimes old beliefs are too difficult to remove: some clients may be unwilling to unwind their old beliefs because they have become such an integral part of their being. A therapist might view the old beliefs of such clients as an important facet of their personhood and therefore as something that should be worked with and not cut away or covered up.

THE GROUP AS A RESOURCE FOR NEW BELIEFS AND MEANINGS

It seems reasonable to expect that if individuals first draw their perceptions and meanings from their family, they might discover within a group therapy system new beliefs and meanings as fellow group members help them define new resources within themselves. Thinking of the solution focused family-of-origin group as a resource for new beginnings and meanings allows the group client to experience new meaning from those whose intentions are positive. It is important in this group setting for the group therapist to set the stage for a different type of conversation.

The following exercise, an exercise in "gentle persuasion," may be helpful for the therapist to use in a new group setting where clients are stuck in old beliefs that maintain unproductive, unhealthy behaviors and are having difficulty exploring their strengths and resources. Groups for survivors of sexual abuse, anxiety, violence, substance abuse, and trauma may benefit from this exercise if it is introduced as a new way for members to visualize their lives and move forward.

The therapist begins the exercise by encouraging members to introduce themselves and then briefly describe their reason for coming to the group and the goal they hope to reach. The idea of this exercise is to assist clients in identifying the source of their current unhelpful beliefs and then in brainstorming with the group for new beliefs, which are based on the perceptions of healthier members, that might be more productive.

In order to help group clients identify the influence of family members on their belief systems, the therapist draws on a large chalkboard three columns, labeled PERSUADER, MISTREATMENT, and RESPONSE, and gives the following explanation:

> Many of our beliefs about ourselves are the products of how people treated us as we grew into adults. [*The therapist may at this point share a personal belief that developed during childhood.*] Sometimes those beliefs keep us stuck, yet we can't just stop believing them. That's okay. We just have to gradually

change them into more productive ideas. I've drawn three columns on the chalkboard. In the first column, I'm going to write down the people in your lives who somehow mistreated you in a way that caused you to believe unhealthy things about yourself. In the second column I will write a phrase that describes the mistreatment, and in the third column I will write your response, which includes the behaviors, beliefs, and thoughts about yourself as a result of the persuader's mistreatment.

After a few minutes, the chalkboard will look something like this:

Persuader	Mistreatment	Response
Father	criticized me high expectations never listened to me	I criticize others easily. I feel shy, have no friends. I don't express my feelings well.

When the exercise is completed, the therapist asks group members, "Is there anyone here who *wants* to keep these beliefs?" The therapist then erases the board, saying simultaneously, "From the descriptions we have written down here and from the introductions you have heard, look around at the members in the group and tell me what you and your peers missed out on as a result of being trapped in the old beliefs.

The therapist encourages lots of conversation at this point and writes on the chalkboard a paraphrase in general terms of what each group member says he missed out on. For example, if a member says, "I missed out on feeling protected by my father because he drank," the therapist would write the word *protection*.

After group members have had the chance to offer examples of what they missed in their lives, the therapist asks, "What do you deserve now, instead? What do your peers deserve?" The therapist continues to ask group members to describe what they deserve today. The purpose of this discussion is to assist the clients in self-actualization.

In the next part of the exercise, the therapist leads the group in a discussion of the importance of mentors. The therapist begins this discussion by saying to the group:

For many of us, there is at least one person in our past who believed that we could accomplish something of importance. That person might have been a best friend, a grandparent, a teacher, a minister, or even a mentor in a community project. It could be anyone who made a difference to how you felt about yourself. Let's spend a few minutes identifying those persons who saw something important and wonderful in you.

The therapist again draws three columns on the chalkboard, using the headings MENTOR, TREATMENT, and RESPONSE, and gives the group the following explanation of the columns:

The mentor is the person who went the extra mile to help you feel good about yourself or about something you did. This person listened first, acted second. She or he considered your feelings and ideas. You enjoyed being around this person. In the treatment column we will list the mentors' methods of interacting with you, methods that positively reinforced your good feelings and beliefs in yourself. What did your mentor do, exactly? In the third column, the response column, we will list the behaviors, actions, and beliefs you had after experiencing the influence of your mentor.

After a few minutes, the chalkboard will look something like this:

Mentor	Treatment	Response
Aunt Anna	always sent me cards	I wanted to be close to her. I felt worthy, open.
Mr. Rob (teacher)	always seemed interested in my ideas	I felt validated, productive, proud.
Mrs. Gray (neighbor)	hired me to mow her lawn; always praised my work	I felt important, energized.

The therapist then leads group members in a discussion of the influence of mentors on their lives. Below are some questions the therapist can use to stimulate such a discussion:

As you listen to your fellow group members talk about their experiences with mentors, what do you see in their behavior that suggests how these positive influences made such a difference in them?

As you look at the list of treatments here, what do you think your mentors saw in you that your persuaders missed?

Given the chance, what would you tell your persuaders about how you want your life to be in spite of their treatment?

On a scale of 1 to 10, where 1 means you are stuck in old beliefs and therefore unproductive actions and 10 means you are free from old beliefs and are acting productively, rank how productive you are in your life, based on the beliefs given to you.

Does anyone disagree with anyone's placement? If so, tell us where you think that person needs to be and why.

Do you think that the negative persuasions led you into beliefs that helped you to act productively or unproductively?

Over the next week, what mentor beliefs about you would you like to take with you to use instead? How will you do that?

What do you hope other group members believe about themselves during the next week so that their week works better?

Glancing over the list of mentors and their treatment of you, where would you imagine yourselves being on the scale when you begin to act according to how the mentors saw you?

Helping clients identify the resources in their family and recall the influence of their mentors enables them to see the evolution of their own resources and strengths and can lead to a realization that such strengths were in them all along. The group can assist its members in identifying strengths, meanings, and beliefs and in identifying which resources seem to work best to change a member's current story. By enacting new behaviors in the group setting, members begin the process of eliminating negative behaviors and, hopefully, modeling new behaviors for the next generation.

SOLUTION FOCUSED FAMILY-OF-ORIGIN THERAPY METHODS FOR GROUPS

The following summary of the methods described in this chapter for helping group members decide on new directions illustrates the goals of solution focused family-of-origin therapy:

1. The therapist helps group members focus on "exceptions" to problems and on increasing their behavior options. One method of doing so is to ask group members to watch for different, more productive, behaviors of their peers during group sessions. The identification of such resources and "exceptions" will alter the meaning of each client's personhood. The group experience offers clients an opportunity to practice their new behaviors in a safe environment. Such practice helps them take new actions in their lives more readily.

2. The therapist assists group clients in their construction of new meanings in situations, particularly those that occur during the group process itself. Insight, as well as the small but productive new actions taken with group or family members will promote the rewriting of such meanings. When group members have difficulty in putting their strengths, resources, and abilities toward solutions, they may be exhibiting evidence of problematic meanings and beliefs they hold about themselves and their relationships. The therapist encourages group members to ask the group for the support they were not given by their family of origin so that they can practice new behaviors.

3. The therapist helps group members understand that new meanings must always be balanced by constructive and adaptive new actions.

Balance between action and meaning is essential; otherwise, the client may become stuck in old beliefs or unproductive actions.

RELATED-MEANING QUESTIONS THAT CREATE NEW ACTIONS

Helping clients move from past beliefs into future solutions requires that the therapist ask questions that respect the past yet at the same time encourage the client to reject certain aspects of it in order to push forward and deal with life more competently.

THE SHIFTING BELIEF FRAME: REWINDING THE PAST

Belief systems that are constructed in one generation (the past) are usually present in some form in other generations (present and future). The therapist, therefore, must not only focus on the strengths of the individual in the present but also concentrate on where these strengths were learned in the past. Likewise, the weaknesses and problems that the individual labels as the past are usually found in that individual in the present. The therapist needs to see how these strengths and weaknesses exist together in an intergenerational framework. He or she searches for strengths and resources in the client's past and presents them as solutions for the present and future. Likewise, when the therapist discovers weaknesses, he or she questions how these play out in the present and how the client copes with them.

This "shifting belief frame" not only helps clients see their options but also offers them the opportunity to rewind the belief thread on the personhood and relationship spools. Also, it forces them to take responsible account of how they construct their beliefs concerning their personhood and their relationships with others.

SEARCHING FOR EXCEPTIONS: QUESTIONS TO FAST-FORWARD TO THE FUTURE

In encouraging clients to search for "exceptions" in their past and present behaviors, it is often helpful to direct their attention to the future. The following are examples of situations and questions the therapist might pose to group clients to "fast-forward" them into the future with the intention of helping clients to set future-oriented goals. As the clients visualize future conversations with significant others, the clients are able to discuss in group how different they hope their lives will be. The following questions are especially helpful for parents in groups who wish to change their image in their children's eyes. The questions and follow-up discussion can be encouraged by the therapist to focus on tasks that could be done by clients to create a new *Legacy.*

> It is twenty years in the future. Your daughter confronts you on an issue related to her childhood that she does not understand. How do you hope you would respond? What would you hope you would be doing afterwards? How might that same technique be helpful with your own parent at this time?

Another discussion to follow these questions would be one that assists group clients to identify beliefs which were developed through parent-child relationships. The following two questions help group clients to identify weaknesses demonstrated by their current behavior. After analyzing their own behaviors, clients can help their group peers to identify behaviors that occur in group. The discussion can then be redirected by the therapist toward one of the clients' developing new behaviors which may change their parents' beliefs toward them.

> When you believe in yourself the way your [mother] did, with the weaknesses that interfere in your life, what behaviors occur?

> When you look at your resources instead of your weaknesses, how might your living these resources more *fully* contribute to new beliefs of that person toward you?

The therapist might consider asking group members to imagine a future where they have retaught people from their past to see them differently. Encourage group members to describe how they would treat their children, spouse, friends, and co-workers when they interacted with them that would be very different. Remember to use the word *when* instead of *if*. The use of *when* keeps the group in a future context and covertly suggests that the change *will* happen.

The therapist might ask group members what they think certain people from their past would need to see them doing differently that would change their perceptions of them. The group might be asked what they think a particular member's family of origin would be seeing in him that would change its beliefs about him. The therapist can ask the group to describe the behaviors that member displays in group sessions that impress them. Group members' responses to this question can be written on the chalkboard. Such a summary of new behaviors is motivating and stimulating when visualized by the entire group. The therapist can pose the following questions to the client being discussed by the group:

How have you been able to change your behaviors here?

What are you believing about yourself here in group that helped you to change? What's going on that made the difference?

I wonder what will happen when you begin to use these new beliefs, in a small way, with your children, spouse, friends, and co-workers just until we meet again?

How do you hope your children will describe you twenty years from now to their spouse and children?

CONCLUSION

The assumptions and strategies in this chapter allow the solution focused family-of-origin therapist to combine two familiar models of therapy to enable clients to use their strengths and resources in the present and future and to examine their beliefs about themselves and their relationships, which are a legacy from their past. In addition, the therapist points out to clients that efforts to deal ineffectively with one generation (usually the past) will probably be ineffective with another generation (usually the future). Clients are encouraged to model their new behaviors for both the older and younger generations, behaviors that have developed as a result of acquiring new beliefs. The therapist encourages clients to examine their past beliefs about their personhood and become aware of the inner resources that can be tapped to enable them to work more efficiently in the present. The therapist is more likely to lessen defensiveness concerning the past by gently encouraging clients to explore contaminating past beliefs while slowly experimenting with new beliefs that can lead to a healthier, happier, and more productive life.

7 Parenting Groups That Work

A mother is not a person to lean on but a person to make leaning unnecessary.

—Dorothy Canfield Fisher, *Her Son's Wife*

In the past, parenting groups were designed to be psychoeducational and therapeutic interventions for improving parenting skills. Full of curricula designed to teach the unskilled, inexperienced, or unsuccessful parent, the groups consisted of experts teaching parents how to be more effective with their children. Parents were given information and were expected to try out new techniques at home on their own children. Sometimes the techniques worked. Other times the strategies did not work because they were applied to children by parents who found the strategies foreign to their personal beliefs and abilities.

Even though the experts said the techniques would work if applied correctly, parents seldom continued using those techniques that did not fit with their personality. Eventually, the stickers on the refrigerator that once seemed like such a wonderful idea were forgotten. The play money for kids who completed their chores on time was misplaced. The time-out that seemed so logical in the parenting meeting was refused one last time by the eight-year-old, and the parents decided that the crying was impossible to withstand. And then there was grounding. This strategy seemed like such a logical solution for the adolescent daughter who arrived home late from a date, but it broke down communication between her and her parents when the school dance came along and she was not allowed to go. The inflexibility and the lack of interpersonal magic in the recipe strategies made it difficult for parents to follow through with the prescribed interventions. The element of inflexibility did not allow for exceptions to the rule. It just did not seem to be a loving, caring, and respectful way to run a family.

I DID IT MY WAY

Solution focused brief therapy assumes that people should develop ideas and strategies for their lives without having a therapist *do* therapy *to* them. Likewise, in solution focused group therapy for parents the ideas and strategies are developed by the parents themselves. Group sessions offer parents the following opportunities:

- An opportunity to look at their experiences in their family of origin for "exceptional" parenting behaviors that made even the slightest impression on them as positive as they were growing up.
- An opportunity to see how they have been successful in the past with their own children in certain situations and to begin understanding how they produced those successes.
- An opportunity to deduce, from examining times when parent–child interactions worked, which parental strategies work for them.
- An opportunity to think about their children differently, so that they can react more effectively during stressful situations.
- An opportunity to feel successful after recognizing that they too can be experts on parenting and can rely on themselves for the answers they need.

A colleague of mine, Stephen Chilton, M.S., facilitates a solution focused group for the parents of adolescents in an outpatient day program in Texas. Below are some of the assumptions Chilton (1997) discusses with parents during the first group session in an effort to help them perceive their job differently. Notice the simplicity and respectful quality of each assumption:

- Parenting is the most difficult job you will ever love.
- You deserve the same love and respect you give to your child.
- Parenting is a continuous call to learn about the best and worst in yourself.
- As a parent, "the love you take is equal to the love you make" (p. 1).

Chilton's parenting group meets for six weeks, and during that time parents learn more about their own personal competencies than they do about changing their teen's behavior. In fact, changing their teen's behavior is not the focus of the group at all. Chilton's goal for the group is to help parents realize that they can become more skillful when they perceive their adolescent differently *and* when they see themselves as a very competent and important part of their teen's life. This can be a difficult task, for most of the parents who attend feel rejected, frustrated, and defeated when they begin the group process. However, Chilton has noticed, as the group progresses and parents look backward, discovering when their relationship with their child worked, there is an improvement in parent–child communication and solution development. As group members develop more competent parenting skills, Chilton has found that his services are needed less and less.

HELPING PARENTS TO BE EXCEPTIONAL

We are shaped and fashioned by what we love.

—Johann Wolfgang von Goethe

Imagine a parenting group where members listen attentively for "exceptions" in the stories told by their peers and point out to each other the competencies they hear in those stories. Imagine clients leaving such a parenting group feeling so good about themselves that their children and teenagers benefit immediately. It can happen.

When I wrote *Parenting Toward Solutions* (1997), it became obvious to me how complicated, restrictive, and conforming *prescribed* parenting strategies were and how such strategies were the only ones available then to the literate parent! Those *recipes* for strategies in parenting manuals based on principles of behavioral or cognitive therapy listed rote responses that were very consistent—and yet very inflexible, because they did not allow for individual differences in people. The manuals seemed to miss the fact that parents sometimes feel an emotional need to give in to a child, that when parents see their child in need they want to do more than is prescribed in a book. The techniques seemed to remove the emotion of love—and kids felt it! For the parent who is organized, consistent, and assertive, the techniques probably worked very well. But not all parents have these qualities. Besides, the behaviors described in the manuals were connected to specific causes, and the responses were written to take care of those behaviors. Perhaps the responses were quite effective with the child or adolescent who rarely gets in trouble. But for troubled children and teens who do not feel they are a priority in a parent's life, who feel unheard and unloved or who are left alone too often, such rote responses can be an insult and can be interpreted as a sign that the parent just doesn't understand or care.

The initial idea for *Parenting Toward Solutions* came to me three years ago while I listened to a mother and her seventeen-year-old son talk very loudly at each other as they told me about their relationship:

TIM: She's always on my back about something. If she would just lay off and stop griping at me all the time about school and working—

MOM: And he's so rude to me. Now if I were one of his friends, things would be different. If he only treated his family as well as he treats his friends—

TIM: Mom, if my family treated me as well as my friends, it would be different for me too.

Using their own words as inspiration, I proposed that we discuss how things would be different if Mom and Tim tried an experimental week of interacting with each other only after thinking first to themselves of how they might treat a friend. In short, I was proposing that they teach themselves new strategies to use to mend their relationship. When I asked them what it would look like when they began to treat each other as if they valued each other in the same way they valued a good friend, the dialogue continued as follows:

MOM: I'd like to be able to sit down with him and tell him my concerns and have him hear them as concerns, not blaming and griping. I'd like us to do things that we used to enjoy together.

TIM: It would help me if you didn't yell and tell me what to do. I really know what I'm supposed to do, so you don't have to tell me—that makes me feel like a baby. My friends cut me some slack and don't push so hard, yet I do what they need me to do.

LM: What do they do that keeps you doing what they need?

TIM: They act like they like me. They talk to me and ask my opinion about stuff.

MOM: I'd like to be listened to like that. There are many things I like and love about you, and I don't think you like to hear that.

TIM: It's okay, but when you yell later, it sort of cancels it out.

LM: So on a good day, when things will be better between the two of you, what will you be doing?

TIM: Talking . . . we used to do that a lot.

MOM: Talking and doing something special together.

Challenged with a new philosophy of how to view each other, Tim and his mom returned two weeks later to report that they were doing much better with each other. There seemed to be less yelling, blaming, and confronting in the house and much more listening. While this account implies that parents and adolescents should be friends, I would clarify that it implies, rather, that they should be *friendly*. When parents use a friendly affect and approach, instead of giving robotic answers to maintain control, they change parent–child dynamics, attend to emotional needs, and lessen resistance and rebellion. As a parent of three teenagers myself (current ages 14, 16, and 18), I can attest to these challenges and to the necessity of tailoring every response to a child's individuality.

TREATING FAMILY LIKE FRIENDS: A GROUP EXERCISE

Making changes in relationships involves doing more than executing actions; it involves changing beliefs about oneself and others. And when people adopt a new belief about something, it takes less effort for them to acquire new actions than when they are just going through the motions of a prescribed behavior. This is why some prescribed parenting techniques dwindle over time. Those prescribed techniques that fit and feel natural to a parent are the ones that are likely to be adopted. With this thought in mind, the therapist working with a parent group might write on a chalkboard the following quote by Elbert Hubbard and ask the parents to discuss what they think it means in relationships:

The friend is the man who knows all about you, and still likes you.

The therapist can then ask group members how such a thought might apply to their relationship with their child or adolescent. The discussion might be met with resistance by those who feel that a more controlling approach is necessary in order to stop the negative behavior of their rebellious offspring. Most of the time, such parents have tried those very strategies and are in the group because the strategies failed. The therapist should acknowledge the objections raised but respectfully remind these parents that controlling apparently did not work, because the negative behaviors remained. Doing something different is the order of the day to produce different results at home. The therapist can then introduce the following questions to the parenting group before presenting the first exercise:

Describe a belief that you have about your role as a parent.

How does this belief cause you to react at times when your kids misbehave?

How automatic is your reaction?

Who has been successful with that strategy?

The point of these questions is that what we believe influences what we do. If a parent perceives a fifteen-year-old son to be rebellious, the parent may become defensive as soon as the son walks into the room; the son will then feel the defensiveness and react to it, thus seeming to the parent to be even more rebellious. If, on the other hand, the parent were to think of the son as someone who is learning to express his opinions, but not yet doing it effectively, the parent might respond more calmly when the son walks in—and might even attempt to understand the son's ideas; the son, thrown off track from his usual defensive reaction, might react quite differently.

In solution focused parenting groups, conversations between parents and therapists blossom when parents' descriptions of child or adolescent behaviors reflect a change of thinking, and along with that change of thinking new strategies for dealing with offspring grow and develop accordingly. The members of one such parenting group I worked with were frustrated and angry at their acting-out teenagers. Most parents in the group had used such traditional parenting strategies as rewards and consequences but without success. Their kids attended a day treatment program for depression, anger, school failure, or drug dependency. I met separately with the adolescents to get their ideas about what their family life was like. Each teen cited needing a better relationship with parents as a personal goal. That goal cannot be met easily when parenting strategies get in the way of the relationship.

As the parenting group began, I asked members to describe what they hoped to gain from the group. I then posed the following questions and statements and wrote the group's answers on the chalkboard, which I divided into three columns under the headings DESCRIPTIONS, REACTIONS, and NEW DESCRIPTIONS–NEW REACTIONS.

Tell me how you would describe your adolescents during the times when you are the most concerned, angry, or worried about them. [In the table that follows, the group's answers are summarized under *Descriptions*.]

When your adolescents behave in that way, how do you react to them? [Answers are under *Reactions*.]

Let's suppose that we keep the same descriptions, only this time let's say you are describing a best friend. You have known this friend all your life and you are very important to each other. You have shared secrets, challenges, and even frustrations together. Suppose on this day that you see your friend as having the traits that are listed on the board under *Descriptions*. Remember, your friend is valuable to you and you want to keep this person in your life. How might you react toward your friend? [Answers are under *New Descriptions–New Reactions*.]

Descriptions	Reactions	New Descriptions– New Reactions
Irritable	Become firm, yell.	Think: Maybe my friend had a bad day. Reaction: Stay calm and caring.
Rude	Become firm, retaliate by restricting activities.	Think: My friend is out of sorts about something. Reaction: Ask if something is going on that I can help with.
Angry	Get defensive, argue; retaliate by restricting activities.	Think: My friend might be having a rough day. Reaction: Listen.
Depressed	Tell them nothing is wrong.	Think: I need to be there for my friend, who rarely gets down. Reaction: Listen.
Confused	Tell them what to do.	Support and encourage. Reaction: Give compliments.
Failing school	Yell, worry, punish by restricting activities.	Think: My friend feels very bad already. Reaction: Feel friend's pain. Offer support and ask how I can help.
Using drugs	Threaten, express disappointment, punish by restricting activities.	Think: My friend needs help. How can I let friend know that he/she is worth more than this? Reaction: Tell friend that I care and will go with him/her to get help. Tell friend that he/she is that important.

Notice the difference in group members' reactions when their descriptions of the person's behaviors differ. Whenever I present this exercise to parenting groups, I typically hear parents remark on how simple the idea of redescription is and on how simple it makes the solutions. They are usually quite surprised at their difference in thinking when they imagine identical behaviors in their best friend and in their own child. After discussing this technique as a possible new strategy when parents are faced with difficult situations with their child, I take the exercise to another level by considering the emotional bond between parent and child and making the following comments:

> Imagine that you began to react to your adolescent in the way that you would to a best friend. What would your adolescent probably say is different about you when you react in that way?
>
> After you leave tonight and are on your way home, promise yourself a favor for the evening: Whatever your adolescent does or says, react as if she or he were a very dear friend whom you want to keep in your life for a very long time. Allow your adolescent to see you as that kind, caring friend who will always be there to help, no matter what. Think about doing this exercise, only for this evening, with your significant other as well.

Most parents might agree that their child's trust, love, and ability to communicate openly with them is a top priority, yet such goals are not thought about in times of crisis. Defensiveness and the need to change the unruly behavior is the goal of the moment. Because of these intense feelings, the parent is asked to try and use new conversational skills with their offspring initially for an evening. When the parents return and report a more positive interaction, then the therapist can ask the parents if they wish to continue their success. The point of the last exercise is not to encourage parents to become their child's best friend. The point is, instead, to help parents see how they think about their friend and to encourage them to use that knowledge as a resourceful guide in dealing with their offspring. This exercise attempts to help parents step back and rediscover the relationship skills that currently work with their friends. The realization that those skills can be useful with their off-spring can be the beginning of the development of new parenting strategies that are more compatible with their individual style, emotions, and desires.

The following worksheet is designed to cultivate still more resourceful parenting skills. It can be used in parenting groups to further enrich parents' ideas about themselves and to help them realize that they already possess the tools they need to be successful!

After group members have filled out the personal survey, the therapist asks them to look at their answers for Sections E and F and writes down one goal from each parent on a chalkboard in front of the group. After listing the goals, the therapist glances at the list and asks if any of the goals require skills that group members might already use at work. For each goal, the group member who formulated it is asked to dictate a strategy from work or home that might begin to accomplish it; other group members are asked to participate in formulating strategies for that person by considering the person's profession or interactions in the group. The magic of this process is that new strategies come not only from each member's efforts on his or her own behalf but also from input from fellow members. The atmosphere becomes one of resourcefulness instead of just education. The therapist cannot go home with group members to remind them to look for "exceptions." The practice of searching for "exceptions" in the group process makes a powerful impression on group members as they begin to watch for what works in others and in themselves, discovering skills that were unnoticed before.

PARENTING ADOLESCENTS, BUILDING SOLUTIONS

THE EVOLUTION OF A SOLUTION FOCUSED PARENTING GROUP

The role of the therapist in solution focused parenting groups should be that of a facilitator. When parents discover their own strengths as parents, they are more likely to use those strengths. Karen Rayter, an expert

THE QUALITY SEARCH:

A Personal Survey of Professional and Personal Skills

How often have you found yourself taking extra time, patience, and care in talking with a client or office worker, only to go home later and be less available to your family, spouse, or child? It happens so easily that we barely notice. But what if we thought of our children and spouse as our most important clients? Would we react differently? Probably. In this exercise, excerpted and slightly modified from my book *Parenting Toward Solutions,* you have the opportunity to take a personal inventory of yourself and identify more readily when family life works well.

A. *List below the qualities, habits, and skills required to perform your job efficiently (examples: promptness, organizational skills, inter-personal skills). Next to each quality, briefly note how you manage to show this quality at work with others.*

1. _____

2. _____

3. _____

4. _____

5. _____

B. *List below how your boss would describe your most valuable quali-ties and skills:*

1. _____

2. _____

3. _____

4. _____

5. _____

C. *List those qualities and skills you use when working with co-workers or good friends that contribute to a good relationship with them. Briefly note how you manage to show these qualities in your actions.*

1. _____

2. _____

3. _____

4. _____

5. _____

D. *Ask your spouse (or significant other) to describe your* behavior *when the good times occur in your relationships with your family.*

1. _____

2. _____

3. _____

4. _____

5. _____

E. *How would you like your relationship to be at home with your spouse and children? (Imagine using a video camera and capturing a better relationship with your family on tape. What would you see yourself doing that would tell you that your relationships are better?)*

_____

_____

_____

_____

_____

F. *If you interviewed your children, how do you think they would describe the* ideal *relationship with you? (If you think first of the things they would like you to* not *do, think of how* stopping *that behavior would help your relationship. For example, if the relationship between you and your teenage daughter consists mainly of your telling her what to do, with little other conversation, imagine her saying, "Stop telling me to clean my room." Think of what stopping that request for a short while would do for her. Possibly, it might mean less stress between you and her and might encourage you to build on the relationship first before asking her to clean the room in the future.)*

_____

_____

_____

_____

_____

in educational psychology, currently trains social workers in solution focused brief therapy at Winnipeg Child and Family Services, a mandated child welfare agency in Winnipeg, Canada. A considerable portion of Rayter's work has been in the area of training and consulting with social workers who deal with parent–teen conflict. The social workers had caseloads of parents who were feeling extraordinarily frustrated and ineffective in their parenting. Using *Parenting Toward Solutions* as a resource, Rayter developed a parenting group with a new focus. She asked questions that were solution focused and kept redirecting the group process away from pathology.

The families included in Rayter's pioneering effort had been in the child welfare system for years. They had received a variety of helping interventions, from counseling and consultation, mediation, and psychological assessments to having the adolescent in the care of the agency for periods of time. These parents, by their own admission, had "tried everything, seen everybody" and were still feeling that "nothing worked." They were beginning to give up the notion of ever having a positive and enjoyable relationship with their adolescent.

As a school counselor, Rayter had facilitated various parent groups, from educational and informative ones to support groups. The solution focused parenting group she formed offered a more positive approach than the interventions that had previously been tried with these families. The solution focused approach, combined with the supportive efforts of the parents in the group, provided an optimistic perspective that more traditional problem-solving therapies sometimes fail to capture. What was different in the solution focused parenting group was that the group did not become bogged down in a contagious negative recollection of past disappointing experiences. Instead, there was a more hopeful exchange of future possibilities and positive parenting strategies, which gave these clients a much-needed sense of empowerment in their roles as parents. This conceptual framework, of envisioning possibilities for a different future, was helpful to parents who were feeling overwhelmed, hopeless, and fed up. In the following section Rayter presents the general format she developed for the solution focused parenting group.

THE PROGRAM

by Karen Rayter, M.Ed., Psych.

The format of Parenting Adolescents, Building Solutions, a six-session solution focused parenting group, was designed to provide facilitators with a structure that encouraged group members to make therapeutic decisions, that set a climate in which members were able to envision a different future for themselves through their own creative ingenuity, and that guided parents in a hopeful way through difficult parenting issues. The program is based on the following elements:

- Family wellness—The program recognizes that parent–teen conflict is normal and that effective solutions are within reach.
- Strength-based—The program, which is not problem-based, allows parents to focus on their strengths and the strengths of their children rather than on the deficits of each.
- Optimistic viewpoint—The program is based on hope, allowing parents to see beyond the immediate problems.
- Hands on and realistic—The program creates an opportunity to build solutions based on the skills, resources, and abilities that parents already possess and that have worked successfully for them.
- New parenting strategies—The group experience provides new possibilities for solutions that fit the experience of the parents.

How the Program Began

Rayter and her colleagues facilitated two separate parent groups from Winnipeg Child and Family Services, East Area: one in a rural setting and one in the city. There were two facilitators for each group. My reflections on the experience of facilitating Parenting Adolescents, Building Solutions are detailed below and are based on my observations as a facilitator as well as on what parents told us as we moved from session to session.

The Target Group

In reviewing the caseloads of the social workers, we decided that each group would consist of parents with similar-age adolescents. Having parents with comparable serious parent–teen issues provided for a homogeneous setting. Much of the caseload consisted of parents of thirteen- and fourteen-year-old boys and girls, many of whom had been in the care of the agency at one time or another. None of these kids attended school on a regular basis, and many were absent from home for periods of time without their parents' knowing their whereabouts. These parents were also concerned about the questionable activities their children were involved in—including drug abuse, sexual activity, gang membership, and various delinquencies.

When potential participants were approached with the offer to join a parent group, it was clear that the type of group we wished to begin held instant appeal for them. Parents were immediately attracted to the idea that only one parent need join, relieving them of the pressure of bringing an unwilling partner. The proposed group was also inviting in that the adolescent did not have to come, therefore sparing a parent from trying to engage a reluctant teenager in yet another round of helping interventions. This seemed a logical place to start for parents, as it is usually they who are most motivated to see things change. Why not capitalize on this energy?

These sessions were clearly a way for individual parents to focus on themselves and on their own ways of thinking, feeling, and doing. They were presented to parents as an opportunity to examine and modify their own assumptions and beliefs about parenting and to understand how unreasonable attitudes might be reflected in their relationship with their adolescent. As well, examining these assumptions would provide an opportunity to evaluate any rigid or stuck perceptions. Through this process, it was hoped that parents would begin to see their situation from a new vantage point and that this cognitive shift would enable them to change their behaviors in ways that reflect their new perceptions.

We expected that as parents began to understand the systemic nature of their own behavior (that when they act in one way, their adolescent reacts in a predictable way), they would begin to see the connection between their doing something different and their teen's doing something different in response.

This was going to be a group not about "who to blame" but about "how to change." It was to be a group not about giving up but, instead, about learning that parents can make a difference in a difficult situation.

The Sessions

During our introductions in Session 1, the initial warm-up question "What brought you here?" was met with a flurry of responses:

"My kid is defiant, unapproachable, verbally abusive."

"There is absolutely no respect."

"I'm worn out trying."

"I've given up."

"This whole thing with my son is splitting up my marriage."

"I'm desperate to find some new ideas."

"I've lost control."

"My daughter does not obey any rules, ever."

"I don't know what to do anymore."

"My son thinks he knows everything, and blames me for it all."

"I can't handle the fighting."

"I can't have my child at home."

"I'm not sure I want my kid at home."

"I'm worried sick about my child."

Additionally, there were questions about Attention-Deficit/Hyperactivity Disorder (ADHD) and various requests for information on adolescent development, blended families, stepparenting, and the whole gamut of school issues. Very quickly, I sensed a tone of desperateness in the air: parents seemed to feel that they were in crisis with their sons and daughters and that there were very few answers. As a facilitator, I saw how quickly these parenting issues could begin a contagious atmosphere where the parents would all spiral downward after telling their story and listening to one horrible experience after another. Yet it was important to be cognizant of the seriousness and emotionality that was apparent. I began what was to become a delicate balancing act, wanting both to let parents tell their story and to move slowly into a more solution-oriented focus.

Conscious of these dynamics in the group, I risked asking the parents to write about how they would like things to be at home, "as if a miracle had happened." The shift from a problem/complaint focus to a future/goal focus was *felt* quickly in the room as the parents, one after another, began to describe the most gentle of scenarios between themselves and their teenage son or daughter. My partner and I were bewildered; parents seemed willing to let go of their painful stories and, instead, to put their thoughts into "what could be." Realizing that a major shift was taking place, we asked parents if this movement was a positive direction in which to proceed. Not only were parents supportive, but they reported a need to be directed away from the more typical therapeutic approach, where they were encouraged to talk only about their problems. These parents had been around the block many times before!

From there, it became our role as facilitators to keep the momentum continuing, toward talk of "what could be" instead of "what is." The full vision of the "miracle" became more real as parents were asked to expand on their version of it and to imagine what their behaviors might be as they approximated this ideal version of home life. Their vision of a better future included parents who examined their own behaviors, an element that, in fact, is required to produce this preferred scenario. As parents entertained their new perspective, it became clear that by holding on to rigid perceptions of their situation, they would continue to act in ways that did not work toward their goal. Thus, the predictable responding behaviors of their adolescents would remain locked in as well. It became clear to parents that change had to begin somewhere. Would they be willing to take the first step?

For homework, the parents were asked to observe anything at all during the next week that might be considered positive in their relationship with their adolescent. My assumption was that parents would typically have one or two stories to relate. There was genuine lightheartedness as parents described their anecdotes of anything that resembled positiveness. One parent related that her son had said "thank you" once. Another told of having her first "somewhat pleasurable" dinner in months, while another parent reported that her daughter had cleaned her room when asked the first time. Parents laughed good-naturedly at what they initially saw as small and possibly meaningless "good stuff."

Given their history of rigid and ingrained perceptions of their children, it was very difficult for some of the parents to admit anything positive. Adopting a positive perspective was new to parents who saw themselves as failures and viewed their adolescents with the same narrow eyes. My intention at this point was to demonstrate that parents had in fact created this "exception" behavior they had reported in their son or daughter. I responded with enthusiasm as we began to investigate how this positive exchange had happened. After a question and answer period, the parental behavior that had indeed created the desired behavior in the teenager was made apparent. The goal of our investigations had been to find the "difference that made the difference"; knowledge of this dynamic allowed parents to view the exception behavior of their adolescent as more intentional.

Once parents began to see and to believe that what they did could actually determine outcome, they more openly and willingly subjected their various reactive behaviors to scrutiny. As well, they were beginning to evaluate whether what they were doing was working. This process was most powerful in that it signaled a slight willingness to let go of unproductive strategies and plant the seed of "doing something different." After all, the thought of their adolescent doing something different in response was a compelling motivator! Yet this was a difficult exercise for parents who had responded in only one way to their child's problem behaviors, with the belief that it was the only way.

The next step was to help parents look at how they could make more of the exception behavior happen. With a new understanding of the ripple effect, that is, of how small changes result in large changes, parents began to determine small, realistic goals. Again, the focus was on changes in parental behavior that could result in a desired direction for the parent–adolescent relationship. With a bit of blind faith, and the assurance that appropriate adolescent behavior would have at least the opportunity to follow, parents were ready to take action. They discussed which behaviors they would be willing to let go of in order to determine if such a change on their part would actually make a difference. One parent was to try to refrain from badgering his son about school attendance, another parent was going to stop driving around all night looking for her kid, another parent would attempt to cap the sarcastic and bitter remarks she aimed at her adolescent.

At this point, it became imperative to discuss what parents might do instead of these typical destructive behaviors. Asking parents what behavior they would substitute for the old behavior resulted in many glazed eyes: they had not ever thought that there were options from which to choose! Having parents focus on what they might do instead kept their energy channeled toward the new behavior, as opposed to just stopping the negative behavior with nothing to take its place. The presence of something (the new behavior) as opposed to the absence of something (the old behavior) was a new consideration for many of these parents.

By the third week, parents were talking about feeling "trained" to look at those behaviors of their own that were producing positive results in their relationship with their adolescent. This was a new way for them to look at their situation. As well, it was quite a surprise to them to see how empowering and enjoyable parenting was beginning to feel. Parents consistently reflected to us how difficult it was for them to expand their perception, to look at their situation with new eyes. At the same time, they felt it was worth it, in that their new perspective was beginning to bring out new dimensions in their relationships.

All of the parents reported that powerful and useful knowledge came from exercises that were aimed at their learning how to reframe their adolescent's problem behavior. Basically, the way we view a situation determines our reaction to it. Thus, if our perception of others influences how we act toward them, then it follows that if we alter these perceptions by redescribing them, we may also change our behavior. For example, if parents redefine *defiance* as "self-protective," *unmotivated* as "not having a reason to get involved yet," and *disruptive* as "not sure how to follow the rules yet," this softer and less accusatory perspective may enable them to reengage with their adolescent in more positive ways.

We applied the same strategy of altering perceptions by redescribing them when our parenting group turned its attention to the serious adolescent behaviors the parents presented: chronic lying and stealing, always blaming others, not taking responsibility for behavior, chronic swearing and verbal abuse, and sexual inappropriateness. Parents began to see that if they looked at their children simply as "liars, thieves, or sluts," it was easy for these labels, which only see the young person from a single frame of reference, to determine their own responding behavior. But when they had an opportunity to look past the problem behavior, to analyze it from another level, they gave themselves the opportunity to understand the motivation and the reasons behind the behavior.

A simple question such as "Why do kids lie?" resulted in parent answers of "wanting to stay out of trouble" and "saving face in front of friends" and "getting what they want" and "wanting to protect friends." The motivation beneath presenting behaviors became more clearly understood. When parents began to think of problem behaviors in this way, they were more likely to respond differently, in a way that was more forgiving and less destructive. Parents invariably got stuck in this reframing exercise when they discussed their son or daughter as someone who "always blames other people for their dilemmas." They were infuriated at the thought of their child never taking responsibility for their behavior in a situation. A lively conversation always followed, with parents openly discussing their typical styles of responding (most commonly, trying to back their son or daughter into a corner of admission, which often escalated the defensiveness of the teen).

Having now had some experience at redescribing behaviors, one mother began to talk more in depth about her daughter's blaming behaviors. As she proceeded, what she discovered beneath the blaming was possibly a genuine lack of self-esteem. It began to make sense to her that because of this low self-esteem her daughter's own survival was her first and foremost consideration when she continually tried to absolve herself of any responsibility. Thinking of the blaming behavior as a survival skill changed the way this mom viewed her daughter. She gratefully talked about what a revelation it truly was to give her daughter this kind of benefit of the doubt.

Changing the way the parents viewed problem behavior offered them possibilities to see their teen differently, relieving them of unproductive thoughts and their own accompanying blaming behaviors. It gave them positive ways to reengage in more constructive ways, as opposed to locking their children into descriptions that shame them and blame them. The description of immaturity became a wonderful frame of reference for parents finding it difficult to reframe problem behavior. Immaturity implies lack of maturity and the message that things will change. Helping parents see their adolescent not as "bad" or "mad" but just as young began to result in behaviors that improved the relationship. Several parents reported feeling relieved, believing that this was an opportunity to let go of anger that they had held on to for so long. They experienced this learning process as a chance to begin a fresh start, one where their energy was no longer depleted by chronic and sustained anger.

Although the momentum in the group was generally becoming one of forward movement, we anticipated and expected parents to speak of setbacks. We noticed that a few parents were beginning to wonder if their efforts were in vain; for these parents there were few perceived gains with their adolescent, and they were beginning to feel discouraged. Knowing that change is slow and often comes in the form of two steps forward and one step back, I did not want to minimize these feelings. To do so would have left these parents not feeling heard as they struggled with the very real concerns that burdened them. Indeed, I felt that discounting these ongoing struggles might perpetuate feelings of failure in these parents who were trying so hard to get it right.

One mother in particular was having difficulties with her teenage daughter. The young girl was still seeing a boyfriend in spite of a restraining order preventing him from seeing her. She was stealing money and various items from the family and her friends. In addition, she was nowhere near returning to school. Her story provided an opportunity for the group to put to work their new understanding of the relationship between a parental behavior (action) and their teenager's response (reaction). The group engaged in a brainstorming activity where they generated a whole list of behaviors that could possibly produce a changed result in the behaviors of the young girl. The mom, according to our brainstorming rules, was not allowed to judge, criticize, or say "yes, but" to any of the suggestions. Instead, she listened intently to the results of the group's creative and humorous ingenuity, which became contagious.

At the end of this session, this mom had a solid plan that fit her experience and personal style of relating. After this validating experience, the mom was able to reflect that although she came to the session with a depleted sense of optimism, she now realized that her daughter had indeed already engaged in some changed behavior. Sheepishly, mom shared that her daughter was now talking to her truthfully about topics on which she would have typically "lied through her teeth." Somewhat embarrassed, she acknowledged that she was now beginning to feel "like my daughter's best friend."

This was an exception that I was ready to capitalize on! To figure out what prompted this honest friendliness between mother and daughter and to support and reinforce it was well worth the effort once the mom saw that things might not be quite as hopeless as she had first feared. The newly-generated strategies from group interactions not only armed the mom with some renewed strategies and hopefulness but also opened the door for the other parents to reexamine their willingness to "do something different" in their own family.

Assigning homework took the form of requiring parents to do something different in their own responses to their teenager, no matter how bizarre or out of the ordinary it might seem. Permission to refrain from their typical unproductive responses freed parents to feel a renewed sense of vigor and courage as each group session ended. Imagine the laughter that ensued as, in the next session, parents related the stories of their new strategies. A mom who found a condom in her son's pocket told us that her normal response would have been to "completely flip out." Instead, she chuckled as she asked her son if he knew when the expiration date was on the package (it was long out of date). This resulted in a humorous and constructive exchange between them about condom reliability.

Another mom told us how her family's rental of the movie *The Cone-heads* over the weekend had resulted in a new strategy for her. When anyone in the movie began to escalate their voice, another would remind them, in a flat, monotone voice, to "maintain low tones." This mom applied the same strategy—with many curious, yet positive, results—to the constant yelling exchanges she and her daughter engaged in.

A father who had enormous difficulty restraining himself from interfering in the fights between his stepdaughter and her mother reported that he was now removing himself to the basement whenever a row began to take place. He admitted that he could still feel his blood pressure skyrocketing but that headphones and loud music were helping. After almost a week of the father's incredible restraint, the daughter, unprompted, told her mom that she thought things were getting much better between her and her stepdad.

Other stories ranged from a mom getting a radio station to phone to get a daughter out of bed, where mom's efforts had only resulted in verbal abuse, to another mom inviting her "totally disrespectful and socially inappropriate" daughter out for dinner with her own "cool" friends.

Injecting this exercise and others into the group was like a breath of fresh air for parents who previously were locked into repetitive cycles and unproductive methods of dealing with their children. It seemed to release them and give them motivation and encouragement in their new-found spirit.

As the group experience was winding to a close, members were amazed at how close they felt to one another and how confident they were feeling as parents. They saw that they had many strengths and resources upon which to rely. In their evaluations of the group experience, there was incredible determination in parents to continue this new and refreshing way of looking at parenting. Surprised at how much fun we had from session to session, parents generalized this learning; they resolved to have more fun with their sons and daughters. They learned that misery and hopelessness did not always have to accompany the difficult times with their children.

The summarizing comments members offered on their experience in the parenting group were enlightening:

"The whole program gave me a brand-new outlook—uplifting and hopeful for the future."

"The experience made me much more conscious of the positives."

"I learned that remembering to look at your own strengths is as important as only looking at weaknesses."

"It has made me feel empowered. I felt sometimes that I was always doing the wrong things with my kids, but I wasn't; I needed guidance to focus on the things that *were* working."

"I realized my daughter has strengths, too."

"The experience allowed me to step back and see my daughter as a human being again."

"I learned that small changes can add up to big ones."

"I now believe that change is possible."

"I realized that my child is worth saving."

"This group helped me to realize that I was just as much a part of the problem as my kid, but now I know what to do instead."

"It made me feel better about myself and to believe that the light at the end of the tunnel is not always a train."

The following letter was received from a parent:

Many thanks for allowing me to share your wisdom and strengths. This class has given me hope, once again, when I was beginning to see none. The last six weeks have made me look at my abilities and behavior, and hopefully has opened some doors that were closed when we began. Thanks for making a difference!

Participation in our parenting group became empowering for the group members, who had experienced only failure in the various interventions they had previously tried, as they began to witness rapid changes in their own sense of self-worth and of personal power as a parent in affecting constructive change in their adolescent. One parent's response alone gave me the proof needed to continue these groups. She wrote, "This group gave me the opportunity to love my kid again."

You may contact Karen Rayter directly in Winnipeg by calling 204-475-7872, or writing to her at:

Karen Rayter
Counseling and Consultation
#201-55 Nassau Street North
Winnipeg, Manitoba
Canada
R3L 2G8

CONCLUSION

I am honored to include this account of Karen Rayter's program in this chapter. Her ability to transfer solution focused ideas into a challenging parenting group is admirable and exciting. She has convincingly described the attraction of the solution focused model for parents who are desperate to try something new and once again feel a part of their child's life. I hope this marvelous example of using solution focused questions, atmosphere, and creativity will motivate other therapists to use this approach to touch the lives of parents in need of solutions.

8 Solution Focused Groups Unlimited

The first and great commandment is,
Don't Let Them Scare You.

—Elmer Davis

Whenever I present workshops to therapists, I am invariably asked the following question: "Okay, but can solution focused brief therapy be used with *this* type of situation?" When I hear this question, it reminds me of how simple the solution focused model is and yet how difficult it is when learning it to believe in its simplicity and flexibility. In individual and group therapy sessions, therapists often hear difficult, complex, and even dangerous problems, problems that can seem insurmountable to both therapist and client. It can be, at times, difficult to imagine *not* exploring the pain that is being described to us. It is helpful for therapists new to the solution focused approach to remind themselves that even if they did explore that pain, it would then simply have been explored (and, perhaps, understood a bit) but not diminished or removed by a solution. People would still walk out of therapy with the same problem, though maybe with a little new understanding. Exploration is also risky, since more harm seems to be done when therapy opens up old wounds, leaving therapists with bandages much too small to cover what sometimes can be a lifetime of pain. Instead, it seems more respectful to listen and acknowledge clients in whatever context they bring to therapy and to view them as having coped thus far, no matter what their complaint. It is this sort of thinking, not the technique, that makes the solution focused model work for the client.

For example, if I think of a client as being forever scarred, I will fall into a problem focus that will leave both of us overwhelmed as we work diligently to erase something that can never be erased. This happens frequently when therapists hear very sad stories. What is more difficult is to sit back and try to observe the client in front of us *differently* as the personal history is told. When I talk with clients during a group session, I am curious about many things besides what brought them to therapy. I ask myself the following questions:

- How is the person dressed? Appearance is important because it reflects how people care for themselves.
- Who sent or brought this person to therapy? The answer reveals information about the relationships of pressures in a client's life.
- Is the person still working, going to school, or continuing activities that are important? This question establishes the client's motivation in spite of the problem.
- Is the person communicating well with an employer about the issue or the need to make changes? This question addresses the subject of honesty and the client's desire for personal change.
- What is going well in the other areas of this person's life? This question identifies what the person continues to do or experience in spite of the problem.

Answers to these questions, which are revealed as the client talks, help me find ways in which the client can begin capitalizing on "exceptions." The client gives me direction as to where I can begin focusing and complimenting. A simple exercise for novice solution focused group therapists would be to apply to themselves the questions repeated throughout this book. For example, the next time something goes wrong, no matter how small, ask, "When is it that this bad thing does *not* happen?" It may be interesting to therapists to look back over the week or month for the same sort of situation that had a different result. The answer is there somewhere, for no one experiences a problem continuously. As Cade and O'Hanlon (1993) put it:

There are times when a difficult adolescent is not defiant, when a depressed person feels less sad, when a shy person is able to socialize, when an obsessive person is able to relax, when a troubled couple resolves rather than escalates a conflict, when a bulimic resists the urge to binge, when a child does not have a tantrum when asked to go to bed, when an over-responsible person does say no, when a problem-drinker does contain their drinking to within a sensible limit, etc. (P. 96)

When I talk with a group of sexual abuse survivors, for example, and hear their stories and the impact of the event on their lives, the atmosphere becomes heavy with heartbreak, scars, missed childhoods, ruined relationships, and self-doubt. Rising above the roomful of sadness by using questions that attempt to take the entire group away from the sadness is like giving the group a breath of fresh air. During those times, it seems better for the therapist to think not in terms of "Can I use solution focused brief therapy in this group because these people seem so sad?" but instead "How would solution focused assumptions assist this group in moving forward?"

In this chapter I present several diverse group situations and offer specific questions that solution focused therapists can use with such groups. Notice how I use the power of group dynamics to work with solution focused questions and how, instead of asking group members only direct questions, as is done in individual therapy, I often ask the group as a whole to comment on what a member is saying.

GET A LIFE! (CASE STUDY)

The following dialogue is from a women's relationship group, a group whose members tried to assist a woman who continued to focus on her problems in spite of the group's focus on solutions. Her reason for coming for group therapy was to find answers after her husband left her and their small son, yet she replied negatively to most of the group's comments, as is clear from the following excerpt from the transcript of the group session:

KIMBERLY: I am just so tired of my life—I have no life. All I do is go to work, sleep, get up, go to work, pick up the kid, take care of the kid, and then go to sleep. It never ends, and it is just not fair that he gets to go off with that cute young thing and make a life for himself without all the responsibilities.

LM: What would everyone in here probably see Kimberly doing when she begins to have a life?

JOANN: I think I would see her going out once a week.

KIMBERLY: I don't have a baby-sitter.

SARAH: I think you need a life. You have to take it if you want it.

KIMBERLY: How? He *has the life, not me.*

JOANN: You know, every time we give you a suggestion, you don't agree with it. You are full of complaints, yet you always have an answer as to why you can't do it.

SARAH: Yeah, yet you have a job and that's hard, you take care of a kid and that's hard; you said you even mow your own yard, and that's really hard. So you can *do things. It just sounds like you* won't *do it.*

[Kimberly sits stunned.]

LM: Kimberly, what do you think these group members need to hear from you when you come back in a week that would change their minds?

KIMBERLY: I don't know. I'm stuck now.

LM: Joann, I remember a time when you were stuck.

JOANN: I really was. It took a year and a half after my divorce, and now things are so clear for me and life is so good.

LM: What did you do to get there?

JOANN: I forced myself to do something, even if I hated it, once every two weeks. Now, a year and a half later, I go all the time.

SARAH: I thought it was the end of the world when my husband left me. It took a while, but I realized that if I planned an evening with a friend a week in advance, I could look forward to something.

LIZ: I remember when I was still single, no matter what, I went dancing on Wednesday night. Just the anticipation of going out excited me. Kimberly, when was the last time you were excited about something?

KIMBERLY: I can't remember.

LM: I hope you will think about that last question that Liz asked. I think Liz has a great idea. Group members, would it be okay to ask Kimberly to think back over the years when she had a life and then bring that information with her next time?

GROUP: Yes!

JOANN: [To Kimberly] And I want you to do just one little thing for yourself. I want you to force yourself to do it before you come back. You already do that with the other responsibilities in your life. Just do this one for you.

The group process was more effective than ever as these group members used a solution focused approach to help Kimberly see possible ways she could "get a life." In the next section, readers will see how the questions revolving around problem issues develop similarly in problem-focused groups, regardless of the nature of the group, and how people in every situation can benefit from thinking that problems do not occur continuously.

THE PROCESS GROUP

Say not, "I have found the truth," but rather, "I have found a truth."

—Kahlil Gibran, *The Prophet*

The process group is often used in schools, agencies, and day treatment and inpatient programs as a time for clients to talk about their problems.

Clients have different issues, yet all can benefit from externalizing their problems. "Externalizing is an approach to therapy that encourages persons to objectify and, at times, to personify the problems that they experience as oppressive" (White & Epston, 1990, p. 38).

Process groups can work for issues of anger, depression, trauma, sexual abuse, physical abuse, frustration, anxiety, and many other topics. The following questions are typical of those posed by the solution focused therapist to group members. Notice how much simpler it is to talk about problems when they become external to the person.

> What would your life be like without *"the problem?"* Who in your life would be doing things differently when it disappeared?

> How is it that you allowed the problem to place you in treatment? [This question helps clients acknowledge their role in prolonging the problem situation.]

> What is it like when the problem is not affecting you? [This question develops a new focus toward client competency.]

> If you could visualize the problem, what would it look like? [This question emphasizes that the problem is external.]

> How do you sometimes avoid letting the problem take over your life? [This question identifies exception behaviors.]

> If you could write a new chapter in your life, Chapter Two, a period in which your problem is absent, what would be different from the current Chapter One? How would your day-to-day actions and beliefs differ from what they are now? Which characters would you select to be part of your Chapter Two so that the problem does not reappear? [This question stimulates ideas about goals.]

> Thinking about your life in Chapter Two, what are some things that you can do gradually now to avoid the problem for the next week? [This question stimulates clients to imagine tasks to undertake that are small steps toward the achievement of their goals. The therapist may support these efforts by mentioning some of the exception behaviors heard in response to Question 5.]

Who noticed someone in our group who was not bothered as much by a problem today? [By helping the group discover exception behaviors in its members, the therapist not only compliments members on their successes but encourages further development of their competencies.]

A solution focused therapist might assign to a group an exercise in which members one day, any day, before the next group meeting, pretend that they are already living Chapter Two of their life. At the next meeting, group members then report on what they did that made the day more like their Chapter Two. The therapist can begin the discussion by saying, "Let's begin by talking about what's been better since our last session as you began writing a small portion of Chapter Two."

THE ANGER MANAGEMENT GROUP

Anger bothers everyone occasionally. As a method of venting feelings, it can be a healthy release. Sometimes, however, anger creates problems in a person's life, distancing important people. Anger may cause people to threaten physical harm to others and may even push them into behaviors that sabotage their own future plans and relationships. When therapists refer to anger in this manner, they are not absolving clients of responsibility for their actions but, instead, are attempting to present the anger as something to escape from. When people allow their anger to take over, it is they who have relinquished control. By the same token, when they disengage themselves from the anger, it is they who are in control.

In the solution focused anger management group, the anger problem is externalized and spoken of as disengaged and separate from group members. This approach allows members to perceive the possibility of freedom from the interference of anger. As a group exercise, the solution focused therapist might draw two columns on a chalkboard and label them as follows: (1) SITUATIONS IN WHICH I LET ANGER TAKE OVER and (2) SITUATIONS IN WHICH ANGER IS NOT SUCCESSFUL. The therapist then invites group members to share their experiences with anger and summarizes their remarks in the appropriate column. The therapist can then continue with the following questions:

> In what situation would you like to be in control of the anger that sometimes bothers you and interferes in your life?
>
> When was the last time you were successful at being in control?
>
> How did you accomplish this?
>
> What is your plan today, based on what you have told the group about how you handle your anger?
>
> On a scale of 1 to 10, with 1 meaning it is impossible for you to control your anger and 10 meaning you are totally successful in this regard, where are you now? Where would you like to be by this afternoon? [For younger clients, the therapist should refer to a more distant time, e.g., the following week.]

At the next session of the group, the therapist might ask, "What's been going better for you since our last meeting so that anger has not interfered as much?"

FAMILY DYNAMICS GROUP

The system dynamics that evolve within a family dynamics group can give families the opportunity to identify competencies in themselves while assisting other families to do the same. This group focuses on *how* family members work out problems, instead of *what* causes the problems. The purpose of the group is to solicit examples of exception behaviors, that is, what family members do when family life works. The solution focused group therapist may be challenged by the family conflicts brought to the group session and may need to direct families away from blaming the *identified client,* such as the adolescent, child, or family member with a chemical abuse problem, and more toward thinking of their life without the problem.

The solution focused therapist working with a family dynamics group might make the following introductory remarks to a new group:

This family group is different. Families may have very different reasons for coming to our group. In some families, members are disappointed in each other or possibly overwhelmed by an event that has happened to someone in the family. I would like for us to think of our group as offering an opportunity to process ways of ridding your family of the *problem* that has intruded into your family life. Keep in mind that this problem, and *not* any person in your family, *is* the problem. Problems are maintained in families and relationships by the things we do or say. In this group, I would like to help you learn how to focus on ways to finally say good-bye to the problem that brought you here.

After this introduction the therapist poses such questions as the following for discussion:

Let's imagine for a moment that we are able to fast-forward through the next six weeks to a day when our group time is over. What would be going on then in your family that would tell you that the time spent in our group was worth it? [This question is an attempt by the therapist to encourage group members to set goals.]

Change in which family relationship would make the biggest difference in your family life? Who would be doing, saying, or acting differently in that relationship? [This question is an attempt to stimulate family members to imagine initial tasks that can serve as first steps toward achieving their family's goal.]

What will be the first sign, over the next week or two, that your family life is getting better?

As the group proceeds to process these questions, the therapist may occasionally solicit other group members' ideas by asking:

Who has changed a family relationship or a relationship with a friend by changing their own behavior first?

How were you able to change your behavior?

Often, group members will state what they *don't* want to keep happening. When they do, the therapist can continue to redirect the focus of the conversation by saying, "Okay, that sounds reasonable. What would you want instead? What will it look like when what you don't want stops happening?"

A good way to end a session of a family dynamics group is by using the scaling question (de Shazer & Lipchick, 1988, pp. 105–117). This question helps the family feel the progress that they have made during the group session, and it helps the therapist know how the group is working. Final questions to ask group members before the session adjourns are as follows:

On a scale of 1 to 10, with 1 meaning very unsuccessful and 10 meaning highly successful, where would you score your family before we met today? Where would you place yourselves now that our group time is over?

What did we do in here today that you liked or appreciated? I am interested in what you think made a difference, if any, so I can continue to do what works for you.

A good question to use at the beginning of the next group session of a family dynamics group is this: "What has been better in your family since our last session that you would like to continue doing more of?"

THE A.M.–P.M. PROCESS GROUP

It is thus with most of us; we are what other people say we are. We know ourselves chiefly by hearsay.
                    —Eric Hoffer, *The Passionate State of Mind*

Daily goal setting is a way of trying to achieve in a short time things that are immediately important to us. In many day treatment or inpatient treatment programs, process groups meet daily, both early in the morning and in the evening. The group therapist can duplicate the following worksheets for use with these clients during treatment (and can give them to clients after discharge, so that they may keep themselves on track as they did during treatment).

A SCHOOL GROUP FOR CHILDREN AND ADOLESCENTS

Children (ages eight to eleven) and adolescents are often sent to counselors for school problems by teachers who want the students to change their behavior. Acting as a facilitator for a group of such students is a difficult task, for the students are often quite upset about being sent to the counselor and tend to blame the teachers for everything. When this happens, the solution focused group therapist can become the student's best ally! Children and adolescents feel most comfortable when they are accepted and their feelings are validated. When a group member needs to blow off steam, the therapist must listen and then casually remark that the member's concern is valid and understandable. Here is how a solution focused group therapist responded after hearing a boy's complaints against his teacher:

> Ms. Smith certainly does not seem to appreciate yet the kind of young man you really are. We have to do something to help her to realize your abilities. Who in our group could tell us what Ms. Smith is not seeing in Sam?

By asking questions like this, the solution focused group therapist involves the whole group in the discussion when a member has difficulty seeing his own exception behaviors. The therapist also does this by asking others in the group to identify their own abilities and to share with the member how they had coped in similar situations. Observe how the following remarks and questions by a solution focused therapist encourage a group of students to envision themselves as taking charge over their actions:

A.M.–P.M. PROCESS GROUP WORKSHEET

A.M. Group Session
Date: _____
Goal for today (specific and behavioral):

_____

1. *How have you minimally or successfully accomplished this goal in the past, even in other situations?*

    _____

    _____

2. *How would you describe the way you did this? What were you thinking about, what did you believe about yourself, and what did you specifically do that made a difference?*

    _____

    _____

    _____

3. *What would the significant others in your life say you did?*

    _____

    _____

4. *Using one of the strategies from Item 2 or 3, what will you do today to stay on track?*

    _____

    _____

    _____

5. *On the 1-to-10 scale below, indicate where you would like to be by the end of today.* _____

    I am out of control   *I am in total control*

    | 1 | 2 | 3 | 4 | 5 | 6 | 7 | 8 | 9 | 10 |

P.M. Group Session

6. *Look at your answer for Item 5. Did you achieve your goal? Did you come close? How did you do that?*

    _____

    _____

    _____

7. *Who noticed what you did today? Who else? Who would you like to be noticed by tomorrow? How will you do that?*

    _____

    _____

    _____

8. *Did you notice changes in your group members from this morning, yesterday, last week? Help them identify their abilities by telling them during group time.*

I'm here to help you get the respect you deserve. It sounds like some actions have given you a reputation or image that is not working for you. In this group, we're going to talk about how to get respect from certain people at school so that they can begin to see you differently.

- How would you like things to be for yourself in school?
- What would your teacher [principal] say would help that to happen?
- Looking over your school years, when have you been able to do that, even just a little?
- Who in the group has been able to do what this member wants to do? How did you do that?
- If I gave you a scale from 1 to 10, with 1 meaning poor reputation and 10 meaning great reputation, where would you be now at school? [This question is more suitable for adolescents than for children. For the latter, the therapist might lead the group in an exercise that enables children to respond in a physical way: The therapist asks the children to open their arms as wide as possible and says to them, demonstrating, "If open arms means you are being the very best student you can be and bringing your hands together so that they almost meet means you are not being the best student that you can be, show me where you are now."]
- Where would you like to be on this scale when we meet again? What small steps could you take to get there before our next meeting?

The following form can be duplicated and used for each student in the group during the first meeting. The form can be completed by the group therapist or by group members during a group session. It is highly recommended that each student complete a form and give it to all the teachers involved. This effort to mend the teacher–student relationship will help teachers see these students as sincere about changing their reputation and achieving success and will give teachers ideas about how to be more helpful. Further, the suggestions made on the form will serve as new strategies for the school to use to increase the chance of academic success.

SCHOOL SOLUTIONS

Name: _____ Date: _____

My Goal:

_____

_____

What other teachers have done in the past that helped me to behave better in school:

_____

_____

Methods that help me learn best:

_____

_____

Behaviors and new attitudes I want my teachers to notice:

_____

_____

_____ *signature*

GROUPS FOR PARENTS
OF CHALLENGING KIDS

There is but one success—to be able to spend your life in your
own way.

—Christopher Morley, *Where the Blue Begins*

Today's therapists often see children and adolescents in therapy groups. But what about the parents of the child or adolescent? They have struggled with a disrupted home life and their child's school worries and have tried everything to teach their child ways to survive. A group that receives much media attention in America is the group of children who are bothered by ADHD (Attention-Deficit/Hyperactivity Disorder), a diagnostic category in the American Psychiatric Association's *Diagnostic and Statistical Manual of Mental Disorders* (4th ed., 1994), or DSM-IV. When a child receives such a diagnosis, parents are sometimes relieved that they finally understand the root of the child's problem but they are still left with the question, How should this problem be treated? Do they only medicate, or do they provide a structured home life or both? The answers are sometimes easier to find when parents do not feel totally hopeless about the situation. The following checklist was developed from DSM-IV criteria for describing symptoms of ADHD (p. 78). The solution focused therapist for a group of parents of ADHD kids might begin the group most productively by allowing a few minutes for parents to fill out the form.

The therapist might then begin group facilitation by asking the following question:

> On the bottom of the form you just completed, you were asked to count the number of items you scored as 5 and the number you scored as 1 or 2. Who had less than ten items scored as 5? Who had more than five items scored as 1 or 2?

Once the discussion begins, the therapist has an opportunity to be reassuring to parents as they discover that their child may be closer to normal than they thought. To encourage that perspective the solution focused therapist may ask the following question:

SYMPTOMS OF ATTENTION-DEFICIT/ HYPERACTIVITY DISORDER

Please rate each of the symptoms below in terms of the extent to which the behavior is a problem for your child at school or at home. Use the scale as follows:

not a problem   *constantly a problem*

1   2   3   4   5

____ Often fidgets with hands or feet or squirms in seat

____ Has difficulty remaining seated when required to do so

____ Is easily distracted by extraneous stimuli (household noises, music, talking, etc.)

____ Has difficulty awaiting turn in games or group situations

____ Often blurts out answers to questions before they have been completed

____ Has difficulty following through on instructions from others

____ Has difficulty sustaining attention in tasks or play activities

____ Often shifts from one uncompleted activity to another

____ Has difficulty playing quietly

____ Often talks excessively

____ Often interrupts or intrudes on others' space

____ Does not seem to listen to what is being said to him or her

____ Often loses things necessary for tasks and activities at school or at home

_____ Often engages in physically dangerous activities without considering possible consequences (may run into the street without looking, hit another child)

Count the number of items you scored as 5 and place that number here: _____

Count the number of items you scored as 1 or 2 and place that number here: _____

> If you followed your child around each day this week, twenty-four hours a day, in what places, situations, and with whom would you find him or her paying better attention and behaving slightly better? What works in those situations? What used to work?

This question can be the focus of one group session. After the discussion, the therapist can follow up the discussion with an assignment for the week based on the following question:

> If you were to watch your child very closely and notice the times when he or she stays on task a few minutes longer than usual, what would you soon realize that he or she needs from you?

> In your family, which parent is more successful at encouraging your child to complete a task, finish homework, or play politely? What does that parent do that seems to work better?

> In which situations—one-on-one or in a group—does your child get along better socially?

> If asked, what would your child say would help him or her do homework, finish chores, play politely? Using this information, how would you approach your child just for this week, as an experiment?

> Recall times during your child's school career when he or she did slightly better. What type of classroom environment, teacher personality, academic curriculum, lesson planning, and so on seemed to make a difference?

> Which school subjects does your child do better in? How are these subjects best learned by your child? Seeing, touching, hearing?

A SUPPORT GROUP FOR GRIEF AND LOSS

The loss of a loved one, whether a child, spouse, parent, or best friend, is followed by grief and loneliness. To make things worse, people who experience loss are often told "Get on with your life" or "Put it behind you; your loved one is gone! You have to continue living." The human spirit just does not function that way. People come into our lives and leave their footprints. To wash away the footprints too quickly leaves us stranded in thoughts that seem incomplete and disorienting. Our lives are *too* changed; we long for the familiar.

In his article "Saying Hullo Again" (1989), Michael White writes respectfully of survivors gradually getting back into life with the *assistance* of those who have departed:

> Grief work oriented by a normative model—one that specifies the stages of the grief process according to the saying goodbye metaphor—will complicate the situation further, rather than empower these persons and enrich their lives. . . . Guided by this metaphor, I formulated and introduced questions that I hoped would open up the possibility for persons to reclaim their relationship with the lost loved one. (P. 29)

The following are questions developed from White's work that are helpful to group members dealing with grief and loss. To set the pace and the focus for the group, the solution focused therapist might begin the first session with a warm greeting statement such as the following:

> In a few moments, I would like for each of you to introduce yourself. As you do so, I would like to invite you to do something different in this group. I want you to describe to us the person who is no longer here with you in a physical sense, in terms of what you appreciated about him or her. Your description can be short or long, whatever suits you.

The therapist then continues the group process with the following questions:

1. As you think about the person who is no longer in your life, I would like for you to do an experiment for a moment. Look

through that person's eyes for a minute at yourself. What do you see in yourself that he or she appreciated about you?

2. How did your loved one know those things about you? What did you do before to show those traits?

3. What difference would it make to how you feel if you were appreciating these traits in yourself right now?

4. When you think about these traits that your loved one enjoyed about you, what are you reminded of that you are missing doing in your life?

5. What difference would it make to you if you kept this realization alive on a day-to-day basis?

6. What small steps could you begin to take when you think about this realization each day?

7. Who in this group would like to comment on what you might be seeing other members doing as they keep this realization going?

8. How would the significant others in your life today know that you have reclaimed some of the traits and behaviors that your deceased loved one appreciated?

9. If you were to recall the times when your loved one observed your happiness, how would your recollection enable you to get back into life?

10. What difference will knowing what you have just fondly recalled about yourself and your loved one make to your next step in getting back into life as before?

11. As you take this next step, what else do you think you might find out about yourself that could be important for you to know?

12. Who would like to comment on other members' descriptions of themselves today? Is there something different you hope to see in them by the time we see them again?

13. On a scale of 1 to 10, with 1 meaning you are unable to get back into life and 10 meaning you are totally back into life, where would you each place yourself today?

14. Where would you like to be when we meet again?

RELATIONSHIP GROUPS

Relationship groups provide a context for people to discuss their goals in current or future relationships. In solution focused relationship groups, the therapist directs members to envision a time in the near future when a relationship works once again. Recalling successful friendships, work relationships, or family relationships, each group member has an opportunity to learn from an examination of past and current successes and through feedback from other group members. By posing certain questions to the members of a relationship group, the therapist can explore with group members some fresh ideas for building more successful relationships. The therapist may begin the group by saying, *"You are in our relationship group for various reasons. Before we begin, let's take time to introduce ourselves and briefly state what we hope happens in our group."* The therapist then proceeds to ask the following questions:

1. Suppose you woke up tomorrow in an improved relationship. It might be a modification of a relationship you are in currently or one you were in in the past. What would you be believing about yourself in this new relationship?
2. If you kept on believing that about yourself, what would you be doing more of in the current relationships of your life, at work and at home?
3. What would others be saying about you while you were believing this about yourself and acting in ways that followed from such beliefs?
4. Take us back to the last time you acted in these ways in any relationship, a time when you believed in yourself this way. Tell us what you did that made things so much better for you in the relationship.
5. How did your significant other react when you behaved in this way in the past?
6. What would your current significant other say or do if you began to add this part of yourself to the relationship you are in now? [If the client's answer is a negative behavior, ask, "What would it do for you to continue acting that way even though your significant other might be uncomfortable, angry, or frustrated with your behavior?"

For those not in a relationship currently the therapist can ask, "What might a new partner learn about you when you begin to portray more of who you really are? How would that have a different result from your previous relationship?"]

7.   When you think of the types of partners you have had relationships with, what type seems most compatible with you?

Notice that these questions encourage group members to focus on creating beliefs and logical actions that will result in their having more comfortable relationships rather than to discuss what went wrong in past relationships. For example: *"Suppose we were all observing John when he was believing he had a right to stand up to his boss about his project. What might we expect to see him do?"*

Each week the solution focused therapist checks in with each member of a brief therapy relationship group by asking a question such as *"What's gone better in your relationships?"* or *"What's been different this week for you personally? What have you done to make that happen?"* An optional exercise for such a group would be for the therapist to pass out paper to the group and ask each member to choose someone in the group to compliment after listening to that person talk for one session. The members then give their written comments to the group therapist to mail or hand out before the next session. The therapist who offers this exercise should also write a brief note to each group member personally, noting that person's competencies.

THE TREATMENT TEAM

Contributed by Ruth Readyhough, program supervisor,

Hatts Off Farm Program, Ontario, Canada

[*The clinical approach to be used with clients by treatment teams in partial-hospitalization programs or inpatient treatment settings is often decided in staff meetings conducted in a group setting. Again, the premise of solution focused therapy is that when a context is created for clients to see themselves dif-*

*ferently, change can be promoted rapidly. However, such a con-
text is difficult to obtain when the staff is still thinking with a
problem-focus perspective. This was the dilemma that was faced
and answered by Ruth Readyhough, Program Supervisor of a
residential treatment center. —LM*]

At the Farm, we have a sixteen-year-old girl with a history of anorexia,
OCD (obsessive-compulsive disorder), oppositional behavior, running
away, and self-harm. Colleen was admitted to the Farm because she was
in danger of killing herself from any one of her presenting problems.
About sixteen months ago, I received a call at home to meet one of my
staff and this girl at the emergency room. Staff members had found her
cutting on her arms. She had not cut down on her arms but, rather,
skinned her arms. It was not life threatening but quite gory! There had
been a scene at the Farm when she was being placed in the ambulance.
When I first saw her, she was on a gurney and not very cooperative.

I began conversing with her by asking her questions so that I could
understand this behavior. She did not respond at first. Eventually she
said, in an exasperated tone, "I don't know what the big deal is. I've
done a lot worse in the past." In another life I probably would have
dwelled on the seriousness of this behavior regardless of the fact that it
was not as bad as any other time. Instead, I asked her what it was about
this time that was different that allowed her to do less harm. She said
that she just realized that it hurt.

From this point, my staff, Colleen, and I went on to explore this
"realization." The staff and I tried to find answers to the following questions:

- How had she come to the realization?
- Had this realization led to any other knowledge about herself?
- How did she feel about this new realization as a control over the
  problem?

Eventually, I had to stop this line of questioning when Colleen accused
me of sounding like a psychiatrist!

As I think of how I might have helped the staff to become more solution focused with this girl, I am reminded that I believe solution focused therapy is not a way to *do* but rather a way to *think*. If I am going to ask the staff to think in an empowering way with the kids, then I have to think in an empowering way in dealing with the staff. The hardest lesson I had to learn was to let go of power and control and let the staff wrestle with recognizing the old ways and then developing new ones. That lesson had to begin when the girl returned to the Farm, and it needed to continue as the staff, taking a more solution focused approach to treatment, recognized her exception behaviors.

As program supervisor, I work hard to stay in the background. I move in when I need to educate, asking a few questions and guiding the process when I feel the need. For the most part, listening to staff members' ideas and supporting decisions and strategies that fit with a solution focused approach was my role. Scot Cooper is a staff member who had studied the theory behind solution focused therapy but had not applied any of his knowledge until we began treating the sixteen-year-old girl with a solution focused approach at the Farm. He was there in the emergency room when I had asked her, "What was it about this time that made you do less harm to yourself?"

When Scot heard her response, he was encouraged. He spread the word back at the Farm about this new approach and, I suspect, about what this new supervisor did that was so different! Later, as I supervised from a distance, I had him develop a treatment plan with Colleen. He presented it to the team and monitored its success over time—both in respect to the team's compliance and the resident's progress. Upon the girl's return to the Farm that day, we told her that we would start with a very high level of supervision to keep her safe but that she was to come to us when she felt she was ready to take full control over her well-being.

Colleen came to us about three days later and told the staff that she was ready to take full control over her well-being. The staff accepted her word and relaxed the supervision. From this point, Scot and the girl went on to build an elaborate treatment plan that centered on her goal of taking care of herself. Colleen never cut herself after that meeting.

Over the following year Colleen discontinued her medications; established a very satisfactory eating schedule, based on a vegetarian diet; took responsibility for her health care by arranging for her own appointments with her physician when she felt the need; and started in community school. I do not want to suggest that her progress was a miracle. It took a tremendous amount of work on the part of the staff to stay one step ahead of the problem and to think in ways that continued to bring out the girl's ability to control the problem. She is still with us and continues to make us earn our pay. I feel very strongly, as does my staff, that the question I asked her in the emergency room was a turning point for this girl and for the treatment team. Although I had quite a bit of training in solution focused therapy, my staff did not, and this was the first time that we, as a newly formed group, worked to apply our knowledge. We have never looked back.

I am certain that we would not have produced the same effect if I had simply laid out a plan for the staff and then hounded them to follow through. I believe very strongly that the only way to encourage competency in the inpatient group is to encourage competency in the staff group. I do unto them, and they do unto the kids!

DISCUSSION

When treatment teams and supervisors decide to switch from a problem focus to a solution focus, as Ruth's staff did, it seems to help when staff members put down on paper various ideas and observations, so that they may communicate their new orientation to clients. Treatment team members can make individual comments on the form below, and then the form can be copied and given to the client. When the client is a child or adolescent, the parents should be asked to contribute their comments as well. This keeps communication clear and, in the process, encourages a solution focused approach from the staff. Eventually, as Ruth found with her staff, such paperwork is merely a guide: the staff creates the context. In addition, the "Group Therapy Case Notes" included in Chapter 2 can be an organized way of keeping up with success and abilities during the treatment day, so that documenting can be more efficiently geared toward exception behaviors.

MESSAGE FROM THE TREATMENT TEAM

Client name: _____ Date: _____

Dear _____,

As members of a treatment team, we are committed to working for you and with you to focus positively on the future. To do so, we have made comments below regarding your success in treatment.

_____

_____

_____

signature

_____

_____

_____

signature

_____

_____

_____

signature

_____

_____

_____

signature

_____

_____

_____

signature

CONCLUSION

I appreciate and applaud the staff at the Hatts Off Farm Program in their evolution toward a solution focused approach for their clients and themselves. This chapter began with a question often asked at workshops: "Can I use solution focused therapy with *this* problem?" As Ruth Readyhough and Scot Cooper discovered, solution focused therapy is more than what a therapist says to clients; it is a *way of thinking* about people. The groups discussed in this chapter clearly show the flexibility of the solution focused model in any type of group setting. As long as the therapist maintains a stance of eliciting competency of group members by withholding advice, the groups work.

9 Going Outside the Therapy Room: Using Alternative Experiences in Groups

Grief can take care of itself, but to get the
full value of a joy you must have somebody to
divide it with.

—Mark Twain

This chapter is composed of unique innovative contributions from therapists who are making differences with their clients by creating different therapy experiences inside and outside the typical therapy room. These therapists have created marvelous exercises and strategies that exemplify the solution focused model's flexibility. They have stretched the limits given to them by their clients and have been rewarded with the joy that comes from being helpful. I hope this chapter will motivate readers to stretch the limits in their own practice and to welcome the opportunity for the creative interactions that await them in each therapy session.

THE SCALING KIT

Contributed by Janet Roth and Christina Hayes, Social Workers
Queensland, Australia

[*In this clever and innovative segment, Roth and Hayes take us into the world of children and capitalize on their ability to so clearly designate objects that describe the intimate thoughts of a child. Whether therapists use these ideas in play therapy ses-*

sions, in group sessions for emotionally troubled youth, or as individual therapy guides, The Scaling Kit will allow children to tell them more easily when life works. —LM]

Scaling is a terrific way for the therapist to gain insight into what is important to a child and to learn what will make a difference in that child's life. It is a simple yet powerful tool in the therapist's repertoire. It is simple in that all it requires of the child is an understanding of the idea of a scale from 0 to 10, or even just the ability to comprehend the concepts of more and less, or bigger and smaller. It is powerful in its capacity to measure the intangible. Scaling was developed as a way to measure the client's own perceptions, to motivate and encourage clients, and to clarify goals and other important issues (e.g., Berg & de Shazer, 1993). A wonderful aspect of scaling is its capacity to minimize misunderstanding between the child and the therapist; when scaling is used, it helps eliminate the need to clarify differences in meaning. The notion of change is inherent in scaling questions. The use of scaling suggests that change is within the child's control. Children are able to determine what would need to happen in their life for change to occur, and therapists can help children realize that they already know what the next step is.

After working with young children for many years in the United States and Australia in educational settings and in family therapy, Janet Roth developed the Scaling Kit to make abstract concepts like friendship, anger, confidence, fear, and happiness concrete and tangible to young children. The kit is a collection of objects designed to appeal to young children, ages four to twelve, although it has also proven to be fun for adolescents and even adults. The Scaling Kit contains eleven different sets of materials (scales) and comes with a simple manual that contains suggestions on how to use the materials, as well as some background on scaling. All of the scales are brightly colored and interesting and use motifs that are appealing to children. The objects are interesting to both boys and girls and do not reflect any particular ethnic origin. The child can explore the kit and treat it much like a toy chest; alternatively, the therapist can choose a specific set of materials for a group of children to explore.

Children are immediately interested in the contents of the kit and participate readily in unpacking the various items. Further, the sets of objects provide an interactive medium to which children readily respond. The Scaling Kit fits very neatly somewhere along the interface between a solution focused approach and the expressive therapies; it allows fears, anxieties, worries, and so on to be expressed while couching them in a solution focused context.

The child's sense of control is especially significant in instances where sexual abuse has occurred, as control has been taken away from the child. Ten-year-old Sue was presented by her mother because of her moodiness and because her mother was concerned about some notes of a suicidal nature that she found in her daughter's room. On initial interview it was revealed that Sue had been sexually molested about two years earlier and that the case had been unsuccessfully heard in court. Recently, Sue had had some uninvited distant contact from the alleged perpetrator and had been teased by some of her classmates, who suggested that she was responsible for the abuse. During the course of therapy, I* invited Sue to use the Scaling Kit, and she readily agreed. Initially, I chose the "green faces," which are ten small green cloth faces with simple downturned lines for the mouth and eyebrows. These faces became the scale representing the level of emotional distress Sue was experiencing. She immediately stated that when she first came to the clinic, she would have chosen nine of the faces (indicating the depth of her sadness) but that now she would choose only two (indicating that she was feeling less sad). Together we explored and highlighted what had contributed to this positive change. Sue expressed in detail the feelings represented by the two faces, adding that she thought that soon she would only use one because she was feeling so much better—although she expected to have at least one in her life most of the time, as life, after all, is hardly worry free!

This seemed to be an appropriate time to offer Sue the "scale of rainbows." This is a multicolored rainbow whose arches can be taken apart, thus supplementing a therapeutic discussion of goals. Moving

*Christina Hayes

from the smallest to the largest arch, the rainbow can be used to high-light steps toward goals. Each arch contains all the colors of the rain-bow, to prevent a child from being attracted to any particular color. Sue immediately stated that when she first came to therapy, she would have chosen the smallest rainbow and that now she would choose the second biggest. This concrete demonstration of her progress had a very strong impact on Sue. Her energy level, sense of fun, and participation in the session increased noticeably during the time she was involved in the scaling tasks.

Scaling can also be used to elicit the child's view of others or, con-versely, how the child thinks significant others view him or her. Our view of ourselves is in part determined by our perception of how others view us. The Scaling Kit provides ten simple figures of increasing size to serve as a substitute for or adjunct to the following question: "On a scale of 0 to 10, with 0 being not grown up at all and 10 being all grown up, where would your mother say you were on the best day you had together last week?" This question can, of course, lead into a discussion of what the child did to become so grown up and of what sorts of things would be a sign that the next level of maturity (the next-size figure) has been reached.

Since I work in a clinic that provides assessment and counseling for children with emotional and behavioral problems, I have had many opportunities to incorporate the Scaling Kit in my work. Georgia, a nine-year-old, had been attending the clinic for grief counseling since the sudden death of her stepfather. Since the tragic event, she had diffi-culty going to sleep at night, with many nighttime fears related to her own safety; was aggressive to those around her; and generally experi-enced great personal difficulties. We resolved the nighttime issues, and then her mother confided that despite Georgia's hopes, their recent relo-cation to another house had not resulted in the elimination of all of Georgia's sad feelings. Her mother in turn felt inadequate, in not being able to help free Georgia of her sadness.

One of my favorite tools in the Scaling Kit is a *large blue face* with two large beaded eyes and a huge red fluffy ball for a nose. This face has ten glass teardrops placed together in a satin drawstring bag to help chil-dren express and move through sadness. (As a result of playing with the glass teardrops, a twelve-year-old boy with an intellectual disability was able to reveal his sadness that therapy was going to be discontinued because of logistical problems. Chances are that this revelation would never have occurred if the Scaling Kit had not paved the way for such a conversation to evolve.) Georgia decided to call the glass teardrops "fairy wishes," which form when "mermaids blow bubbles, and the fairies catch them, and then turn them into wishes." She had seen these in the local Fairy Shop. Without discounting her explanation, I said that I was going to call them tears, because I was interested in getting an idea of the difference between how things were for her when she first came to the clinic and how they were at that very moment. Georgia readily accepted this description, saying that when she first came to the clinic she would have chosen all of the teardrops but that now she would choose only five. As she arranged them on the face, I was briefly distracted by some tidying task, until suddenly Georgia exclaimed, "Oh, look! I made a smile!" She had, in fact, arranged the tears in a smile on the face. This led very elegantly to my being able to comment that the tears had indeed turned into wishes after all!

Next, we chose the "heart scales." Placing a small plastic figurine on the table, I invited Georgia to demonstrate the amount of love she felt there was in her life. She immediately surrounded the small plastic figure with all ten of the small heart shaped pieces, or Love Hearts, saying that she felt very loved by her mother and all of her other relatives. Later, with Georgia's permission, I was able to convey this to her mother in a way that significantly reduced the woman's anxiety concerning the amount of love she was able to provide for her child.

In the last session, we chose the "green faces," again with my explanation that I wanted to understand the difference between Georgia's sadness before and now. Without hesitation, Georgia declared that initially she would have chosen all ten faces to represent the amount of her sadness but that now she would choose only five. She placed the five faces around the plastic figurine, designating one for her stepfather; one for her grandfather, who also had recently died; one for her pet bird, who had died only a week earlier; one for her mother's baby, who died several years earlier; and one for the "worry" that was there all the time.

The last one she picked up and placed on the head of the plastic figurine, thereby almost swamping it. This last expression, which in another context could have been interpreted very negatively, in this session led to a very natural discussion about the times when worry is actually *not* present. Georgia was able to identify many occasions when worry was completely absent from her life.

Although it may seem to the reader that this session must have lasted for hours, Georgia's involvement with the Scaling Kit took only about thirty minutes!

Some of the most versatile items in the Scaling Kit are the foam blocks, which can be used safely for stacking or knocking down. They lend themselves to other symbolic activities as well. For example, the therapist can ask a child, "If all these blocks are the wall which you have built to keep you safe, how will you know when it is safe to take away just one of the blocks from the wall?" One child, Amanda, age 7, mentioned after building her wall that the first block she would throw away would be "old friends" who were no longer supportive. She literally threw the foam block across the room! Amanda then proceeded to step over her wall, and in doing so she noticed the difference in how she felt without the burden of unhappiness. She was then relieved as well to be able to once again step back behind the safety of her wall. I* was able to encourage her to go slowly and to stay safe as I questioned her about the people in her life who allowed her to feel safe even without her wall. Amanda named and tossed away other blocks, such as resentment, but I suggested that we go at it a bit more slowly, in order to be able to continue to feel safe; therefore, we put the resentment block back in its place for the time being.

The use of the Scaling Kit is limited only by the imagination of the therapist or client. The various scales can be used in solution focused therapy, in group therapy, and in nondirective play therapy and are also a useful tool in narrative therapy for externalizing the client's problem.

*Janet Roth. (Ms. Roth can be contacted at P.O. Box 216, Kenmore, Queensland, Australia 4069.)

ADVENTURE-BASED EXPERIENTIAL THERAPY (ABET)

Contributed by Mike Bishop, Ph.D.
Arlington, Texas

[*If you've ever tired of the therapy room on a lazy spring afternoon and wanted to take your client outdoors for a breath of fresh air and perhaps a fresh perspective, this approach will at least offer you therapeutic reasons to do so! The solution focused assumption "Change the context and you change the behavior" makes sense when the environment is as much fun as it is therapeutic. —LM*]

THERAPIST: So, Cindy, how was your group able to make it across that river of molten chocolate this time, when you were not able to do it in the other four attempts?

CINDY: I don't know.

THERAPIST: Yeah, I know you don't know. But if you did know, what would the answer be?

CINDY: Well, I guess we really believed that we could work together to get the job done. We were able to share the magic marshmallows as a team instead of demanding that we each use them in our own way.

THERAPIST: So, if your family is working together as a team at home just like you did crossing this Hot Chocolate River, what would you be doing?

The above dialogue is an example of Adventure-Based Experiential Therapy (ABET). The dialogue demonstrates how an experiential exercise can combine activities with the therapy techniques and competency based attitude and still offer challenges to body, mind, and emotion. The program emphasizes the emotional and physical safety of each individual as well as of the group as a whole. It values and respects each participant and provides a new and unique environment in which participants learn new methods of communication, teamwork, and problem-solving skills based on individual resources. The following exercise is an example of how solutions can develop from imaginary places in a client's mind.

THE THREE CHAIRS

The therapist sets up three chairs in a row, explaining that the first chair represents life five years ago. The second chair represents the present moment, and the third chair represents life five years into the future. (The time intervals may be scaled up or down.) Therapy group members each have to sit in all three chairs and talk about themselves as though the stage that chair represents was happening just then. Other group members can ask questions such as the following:

Are you happy?

What was your biggest fear?

In which seat did you feel less fear, more happiness?

How did you overcome those problems in the past?

What advice would have been helpful to you then?

WHAT IS ABET?

If you have ever been taken on a walk while blindfolded or have ever leaned back to fall into the supportive hands of a partner in a "trust lean," you have experienced an ABET-type activity. In general, ABET refers to a wide array of action activities, ranging from a twenty-one-day Outward Bound wilderness adventure program to two people pushing on each other's palms in a small office. People often think of experiential therapy as being similar to ROPES* courses, used by many

---

*A ROPES course consists of a series of structures and obstacles constructed out of ropes, cables, platforms, ladders, and poles. The physical appearance of a ROPES course is similar to that of a military obstacle course. The course is designed to facilitate activities that offer a varying degree of involvement, difficulty, and perceived risk. The term "ROPES" has become associated with any form of adventure initiative that is designed as an experiential activity for a group.

residential treatment centers in their programs. Through mental and physical activities and problem-solving exercises, ABET utilizes communication and teamwork to develop new awareness about the participants' behavior while they are having fun. The ROPES program is such an experiential activity for families, groups, and individuals; it involves a series of structures, such as cables, poles, walls, and logs, that the participants must learn to master. The ROPES course itself may look similar to a military obstacle course.

The activities of ABET are designed to enable therapy group members to experience situations in which real-life issues are faced in a different context. These situations provide exciting, thought-provoking experiences that participants may choose to discuss in a group activity called processing, which is a form of reflection. Processing, action, and application are components common to experiential learning. The following technique, called the Solution Box exercise, is an example of how processing items from the kitchen can create a new context for the future:

The therapist fills a shoe box with all types of junk—objects from kitchen and desk drawers and items that usually clutter the top of a dresser, such as stones, pennies, tokens, figurines, and tickets. Family members are each asked to name the qualities, gifts, or resources they would like to bring to their family after their problem is solved or after the problem has lost control over their family. Next, they are asked to find an object that represents that result. The therapist then asks:

> What will be going on during that time in your family that will tell you it is time to contribute the piece of junk?

> What do you think your mother, father, or sibling will be doing that would tell you that they needed to present their junk?

APPLYING IDEAS OF ABET TO SOLUTION FOCUSED GROUP THERAPY

Families, couples, and individuals come to us because they are experiencing problems such as sadness, anger, frustration, depression, or despair. ABET offers fun to help reduce the seriousness of these issues. Even if no apparent therapeutic resolution of the problem is noticed, a period of fun is something that may well be needed by clients in times of such seriousness; moreover, it offers them the opportunity to do something different (de Shazer, 1985). Karl Rohnke (1994) uses the term F.U.N.N. (Functional Understanding Not Necessary) to describe the good these activities can add to the human experience. When F.U.N.N. is experienced, it puts group participants in a different space, experience, or reality, a place they may not have experienced in a long time (or ever), a place where making changes may be possible or easier, a place in which they can feel competent at last.

THE DEMO BOX EXERCISE

The therapist asks the group members to sit on the floor and use the "junk" from the Solution Box exercise to make a visual model of how they see their problem. The members are asked to show how they would someday see the solution and how it translates into behaviors for each person in the group. For example, an adolescent might pick up a broken toy and say that he feels damaged by abusive words. He can then choose another object at the therapist's encouragement that appears strong and complete. The adolescent can then describe how feeling whole would result in new behaviors.

This exercise is very helpful in lessening resistance with children, adolescents, and clients who in the past might have been labeled uncooperative. By stepping outside of "that counseling stuff," even the most resistant adolescents can create and learn new ways of thinking, believing, and behaving when they are having F.U.N.N. The Demo Box exercise offers clients an opportunity to see their problem as an object and is therefore an externalizing technique.

ABET activities allow clients to use all of their resources to create solutions to problems. The activities create stress—a positive stress created in a safe and accepting environment—by putting clients in situations they are not accustomed to and giving them permission to experiment with modes of thinking, feeling, and behaving they have not dared to allow in their comfort zone.

ABET AND PLAY

You can discover more about a person in one hour of play than in a year of conversation.

—Plato

Mary Poppins, an expert experiential family therapist, introduced the notion of kite flying to her employer in order to find his real personality and understand his life goals. When we play and become involved in an activity, we tend to lose ourselves in a trance; it is difficult for us to stay hidden and guarded. Our thoughts and emotions come to the surface in the form of play behavior. ABET activities offer the therapist a way of observing the behavior patterns of individuals and the interactional patterns of families and groups. Videotaping a family initiative and then showing it back to the family has been a very productive way for therapists to get families to recognize their own patterns and then decide to do something differently. The following exercise provides clients with the opportunity for play.

Group Juggling

In this exercise the therapist has the members of a group juggle several objects simultaneously without dropping any of them. Group members stand in a circle, and the game begins when one person tosses a catchable object, such as a tennis ball, rubber chicken, or some other soft, easy-to-catch object to someone across the circle. That person tosses it to someone else, and the tossing continues until a pattern has been established and the object is finally returned to the initiator. Once everyone is familiar with the pattern and while the object is being tossed around, the therapist can add additional objects. Action can become quite intense as group members concentrate on tossing and catching objects. This is a nice exercise to help even the shyest person feel competent and the most frustrated person learn patience.

SOLUTION FOCUSED QUESTIONS
FOR EXPERIENTIAL GROUPS

The following questions can be added to experiential exercises to help clients adopt a solution focused approach to their problem:

How has this problem been a problem before, in other activities, in reaching your goals?

What were you able to do this time in the activity that you were not able to do last time?

How did you get that to happen?

How did you keep from giving up in the activity when it did not work the first time?

Let's say that this activity ends up being helpful for you. How will you know?

How do you explain the way the problem lost its power over you during this activity?

What was different about the period during which you did this activity as compared to the times when the problem is more in control? What was different about you?

Did it surprise you that you were able to get this far in the activity?

How do you explain your ability to do that? Where did you get that ability?

What will be going on when you use the skills you have learned here at home, at school, or on the job?

CREATING ADVENTURE IN THE MIND

ABET encourages us to step into our imagination. In Tolkien's classic tale *The Hobbit,* Bilbo Baggins describes the situation to which many people have resigned themselves: *"We are plain quiet folk and have no use for adventures. Nasty disturbing things! Make you late for dinner! I can't see what anybody sees in them."*

When clients use their imagination they have an opportunity to escape momentarily from problems and experience new solutions. Such experiences serve as a refreshing alternative to complex therapy and help the client feel skillful.

The following books include descriptions of activities that are quite helpful for therapists interested in doing additional experiential activities with their clients: *Islands of Healing* describes the history and philoso-phy behind adventure-based counseling, and *The Bottomless Bag, Again!* describes activities, includes funny philosophical sayings, and explains adventure philosophy.

RETEAMING

Contributed by Ben Furman, M.D.
Helsinki, Finland

[If you've ever been asked to take over a PTA project as a par-ent, to organize a committee in a university setting, or to help a lagging company regain momentum, you've been asked to "re-team." This section will give you a clear idea of how simply the solution focused model can fit into a diverse population in need of team-building skills. —LM]

Companies that have had the experience of working with well-known and expensive consultants say that solution focused therapy is better in terms of being more successful in furthering the development of good relationships among staff members. To perform such a feat, therapists can simply improvise and use exactly the same questions they use with clients. For example, instead of the miracle question, the therapist might want to use the "dream team question": "How will your team function in the future when it functions like a dream team?"

The following paragraphs offer suggestions for therapists who give workshops for business clients:

Allow your clients to set their goals and then choose one of those goals to work toward with them. Ask the clients what the benefits will be of reaching that goal and make a list of those benefits. This seems to increase clients' motivation. Encourage them to think of progress toward the goal as a stepwise process and ask them what actions will be needed tomorrow, in a week, and in a month to reach the goal.

Look at the resources within the company. Capitalize on your knowledge when you brainstorm with your clients in discussing what they desire to add to their expertise. Take the time! People love to be told by others what resources they have. Let them shine! Talk about resources outside the team. No team is self-sufficient. Encourage your clients to look at what we call "exceptions," but don't use that word (it is a solution focused colloquialism). Instead, talk about times when progress toward the stated goal took place during some other project or assignment. Focus on who performed certain jobs best by using questions like the ones suggested below:

Who has contributed to those times?

What about recent progress? Who or what made a difference?

Wow, how did you do it?

When the workshop is complete, the therapist can suggest that a follow-up meeting take place to assess what progress occurred and who deserves credit for the progress. Group members can perhaps elect a spokesperson to observe and report on the team's progress during weekly meetings and during the follow-up consultation. To find out more about ReTeaming and the ReTeaming workbook "Succeeding Together," now available in four languages, visit the official website of ReTeaming International at *www.reteaming.com*

Dr. Ben Furman can be contacted at

Brief Therapy Institute
ben.furman@reteaming.com

HOW TO LEAD WITHOUT LEADING
Contributed by Brian Cade
Sydney, Australia

[*Therapists are entering a period where they must diversify their practice to keep their livelihood. Perhaps you've often thought about consulting and how therapeutic strategies just might work in certain interpersonal aspects of business. In this segment Brian Cade cleverly describes how therapists might approach a business or other organizational setting in an effort to build teams for success. As you read through the steps, notice the competency-based approach that is projected toward those looking for guidance and watch how the exercises promote their development of their own ideas. —LM]*

In my consulting work in various business and organizational settings, I have used a number of techniques and ideas from my clinical practice. Here are some suggestions for therapists who are interested in conducting workshops in such settings:

1. Always focus on specific important functions and goals of the company and on how teams might work best together to perform or achieve them (rather than, as so often seems to happen, use "warm and fuzzy" relationship exercises that bear no direct relation to these aspects of the company).
2. Divide the participants in the workshop into small groups to discuss what is currently working fine and what doesn't need any particular change.
3. Divide the participants into small groups to discuss what ideas and suggestions they think that I, as an outside consultant/expert, will be likely to come up with at the end of the consultation.
4. Divide the participants into small groups and ask them to imagine that six months have passed and that their organization is in great shape. Invite them to discuss what specifically took place during this interval of time that led to team relationships, customer focus, and leadership styles being just the way they need them to be. (The "miracle question" can also be used).
5. Divide the participants into small groups in which members imagine themselves to be employees or customers either now or six months from now. Invite them to discuss what is good about either working for or dealing with the company.

Obviously, the use of small groups depends on the number of people attending the workshop. (If participants represent different levels or disciplines within the organization, I usually mix them up in the small groups.) If small groups are used, the workshop ends with a large group feedback session in which a whiteboard is used or sheets of paper summarizing ideas are handed out.

When the process works well, the consultant rarely has to come up with anything other than validation and complimentary remarks on the participants' efforts. Clearly, it is helpful to have clarified the organization's agenda and participants' expectations before starting the workshop. I usually start by declaring my understanding of the purpose of the consultation and checking that this is what participants agree is the goal of the workshop.

CONCLUSION

Writing a book can be a delightful challenge. This book has stretched many of my ideas about groups and group therapy and has challenged me to continue adapting the solution focused model to many more of the numerous situations faced by therapists every day. I can still see on the horizon more opportunities than ever for therapists to develop their own unique ways of creating opportunities for clients to learn and heal. I hope the ideas in this book help you create a more successful and exciting therapy practice and experience for your clients *and* yourselves.

COLLABORATIVE NOTES: PROMOTING CHANGE AFTER THE SESSION

Blaine Powel
Prince George, British Columbia*

[*Remember the note in your lunch box, the special anniversary card, the scribbled drawings from your four-year-old that stole your heart? Collaborative note taking can create the magic between therapist and client by conveying the message "What*

---

*Excerpts in this segment are from previously published work in the *Journal of Collaborative Therapies,* 1997, 5(1), 18–21.

you say is important." During these hectic days of managed health care demands, time with clients can be limited. In this segment, Blaine Powel offers us an alternative to tedious note taking. His method gives us the opportunity to do two jobs at once—learn from our clients what worked and document at the same time! —LM]

After a busy day at work, Mary rushed to the shopping center to pick up some groceries. From there it was home to cook supper. Supper had to be quick, as her son, Frank, had to be dropped off at his hockey practice. As well, Mary had promised Sarah that she could practice driving tonight for her driver's exam. Later that evening, after Sarah and Frank had gone to bed, Mary finally sat down to relax. She reflected on her therapy session earlier in the day and the discussion around being a sole parent. But there was something else she and her therapist had talked about. Now what was it? Mary remembered that she still had the collaborative note they had written, so she retrieved it and began to read.

But what are collaborative notes? In 1991, Jean Turner, a professor with the family therapy program at the University of Guelph in Ontario, introduced me to the idea of writing notes with clients and then giving them a copy. Collaborative notes are written in the last five to ten minutes of a session and can be used in individual, family, or group therapy situations. Together therapist and client write down the points covered in the session and their thoughts or feelings about the session.

HOW TO INTRODUCE COLLABORATIVE NOTES

Collaborative notes are first presented when the therapist talks about what clients can expect at the first session. At the end of the session, when the note is about to be written, the details can be discussed. The note can be created in different ways: Clients may write the note themselves, they may choose to have none of their thoughts written down, or they may dictate their comments, which are written down verbatim. When it comes to what is written in the note, I inform people that there is only one rule: if they decide to dictate to me, I ask them to talk slow enough for me to write their words down. There are no rules about what they say or how they say it. People may say what they like or dislike, may include points they wish to remember, may reflect on past sessions, or even fantasize about future goals. The information they give may be in outline form, or diagrams may be drawn. Spelling and grammar are not important. In short, anything people want recorded is written down. [What is important is that only client input dictates the note, not the therapist, thus keeping it client-based.]

THE THERAPEUTIC VALUE OF COLLABORATIVE NOTES

Generally, I find that people choose to dictate their thoughts the first few times collaborative notes are made. After they become familiar with the process, some people choose to write the note themselves. Just under 70 percent of the people I work with prefer writing their own comments. Some clients will object to writing their own note. As one teenager told me, "I like you writing down what I say. I wouldn't do it if I had to write it myself." Some statements I use to begin the collaborative note exercise are as follows:

Shall we write our note now?

Will you do the writing this week, or do you prefer to dictate your thoughts today?

What do you want recorded about today's session?

After the client's first comment has been recorded, I might say, "What else do you want written down?"

Reading aloud the note at the next session can help focus clients on where we ended. It is also important to ask if people agree with what is recorded and if there are any corrections or additions they want made; people often spontaneously proceed to fill me in on what has happened since the last time we met. If goals were written down, they can be reviewed at this time.

Since notes do not disappear like conversations, some people continue to read their notes over time. As one person wrote: "When I feel I have messed up again, I go and read our notes, and it helps me remember my good stuff too. When I go back and read about what I was feeling before, I am surprised by the changes I made." Notes may help people focus on the work they wish to do. One person said of her notes, "Sometimes by the time I get home from work, I have forgotten what we talked about, and I find it good to go and read the note." Notes can also help clients evaluate their progress. One person said, "I read the first note that we did a long time ago. Gee, what a change. I guess they help me see my changes, too."

Collaborative notes appear to inform people about their own thinking. People tell me that the notes help them to understand themselves. Others have added that part of feeling understood is being able to correct what I've written if I miss their point. Learning from their notes what people believe is helpful about our conversation is often helpful to me. While some of our comments may be similar, people often focus in their notes on where their views differ from mine. I believe this adds to the "information of importance." In addition, because of the collaborative notes, my case files are not limited to my own comments but include those of the "customer" as well; the notes are a way of adding the client's voice to the file.

REFERENCES

Agel, J., & Glanze, W. (1987). *Pearls of wisdom: A harvest of quotations from all ages.* New York: Harper & Row.

Alcoholics Anonymous. (1939). *The story of how more than one hundred men have recovered from alcoholism.* New York: Works Publishing

Alcoholics Anonymous. (1976). *The story of how many thousands of men and women have recovered from alcoholism.* New York: Alcoholics Anonymous World Services.

American Psychiatric Association. (1994). *Diagnostic and statistical manual of mental disorders* (4th ed.). Washington, DC: American Psychiatric Association.

Berg, I. K., & de Shazer, S. (1993). Making numbers talk: Language in therapy. In S. Friedman (Ed.), *The new language of change* (pp. 5–24). New York: Guilford Press.

Berg, I. K., & Miller, S. (1992). *Working with the problem drinker.* New York: Norton.

Cade, B., & O'Hanlon, W. (1993). *A brief guide to brief therapy.* New York: Norton.

Camp, W. (1990). *Camp's unfamiliar quotations from 2000 B.C. to the present.* New York: Prentice-Hall.

Carlson, R. (1997). *Don't sweat the small stuff . . . and it's all small stuff.* New York: Hyperion.

Chilton, S. (1997). *A parent's handbook: A competency-based approach for parents of adolescents bothered by chemical dependency. (A companion manual for intensive outpatient and partial hospitalization programs.)* Fort Worth, TX: Self-published.

Chomsky, N. (1957). *Syntactic structures.* The Hague: Mouton.

Covey, S. (1989). *The seven habits of highly effective people: Powerful lessons in personal change.* New York: Fireside Books.

de Shazer, S. (1982). *Patterns of brief family therapy.* New York: Guilford.

de Shazer, S. (1985). *Keys to solutions in brief therapy.* New York: Norton.

de Shazer, S. (1988). *Clues: Investigating solutions in brief therapy.* New York: Norton.

Dolan, Y. (1991). *Resolving sexual abuse.* New York: Norton.

Durrant, M. (1993). *Residential treatment.* New York: Norton.

Hargrave, T. D., & Anderson, W. T. (1992). Finishing well: Aging and reparation in the intergenerational family. New York: Bruner/Mazel.

Hargrave, T. D. (1994). Families and forgiveness: Healing wounds in the intergenerational family. New York: Bruner/Mazel.

Heather, N., & Robinson, I. (1985). *Controlled drinking.* London: Methuen.

Hoffman, L. (1981). *Foundations of family therapy.* New York: Basic Books.

Khuel, B. (1995). The solution-oriented genogram: A collaborative approach. *Journal of Marital and Family Therapy, 21*(3), 239–250.

Lipchick, E., & de Shazer, S. (1988). Purposeful sequences for beginning the solution-focused interview. In E. Lipchick (Ed.), *Interviewing* (pp. 105–117). Rockville, MD: Aspen.

McFarland, B. (1997). Swords into Plowshares. *The Family Therapy Networker, May/June,* 36–43.

Metcalf, L. (1997). *Parenting toward solutions: How parents can use skills they already have to raise responsible, loving kids.* Englewood Cliffs, NJ: Prentice-Hall.

Metcalf, L., & Thomas, F. (1994). Client and therapist perceptions of solution-focused brief therapy: A qualitative analysis. *Journal of Family Psychotherapy, 5*(4), 49–66.

Minuchin, S., & Fishman, C. (1981). *Family therapy techniques.* Cambridge, MA: Harvard University Press.

Moore, T. (1992). *Care of the soul: A guide for cultivating depth and sacredness in everyday life.* New York: HarperCollins.

O'Hanlon, W. H., & Weiner-Davis, M. (1989). *In search of solutions.* New York: Norton.

Redfield, J. (1993). *The celestine prophecy: An adventure.* New York: Warner Books.

Redfield, J. (1996). *The celestine prophecy: A pocket guide to the nine insights.* New York: Warner Books.

Rohnke, K. (1994). *The bottomless bag again.* Dubuque, Iowa: Kendall/Hunt Publishers.

Shoel, J., Prouty, D., & Radcliffe, P. (1988). Islands of healing. Hamilton, MA: Project Adventure, Inc.

Todd, T. (1994). *Surviving and prospering in the managed mental health care marketplace.* Sarasota, FL: Professional Resource Press.

Todd, T. (1996). *Brief therapy workbook of exercises and role plays.* Denver: Brief Therapy Institute of Denver, Inc.

Webster's New Twentieth Century Dictionary (2nd Edition). 1983.

White, M. (1989). Saying Hullo Again: The incorporation of the lost relationship in the resolution of grief. In *Selected Papers.* Adelaide, Australia: Dulwich Centre Publications.

White, M., & Epston, D. (1990). *Narrative means to therapeutic ends.* New York: Norton.

Woolfolk, A. (1995). *Educational psychology.* Boston: Allyn and Bacon.

INDEX

Note: Page references to worksheet material appear in italic.